North of Belleville

North of Belleville

haiku

James Deahl

photography

Richard M. Grove

Hidden Brook Press

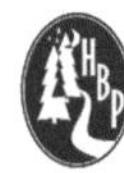

First Edition

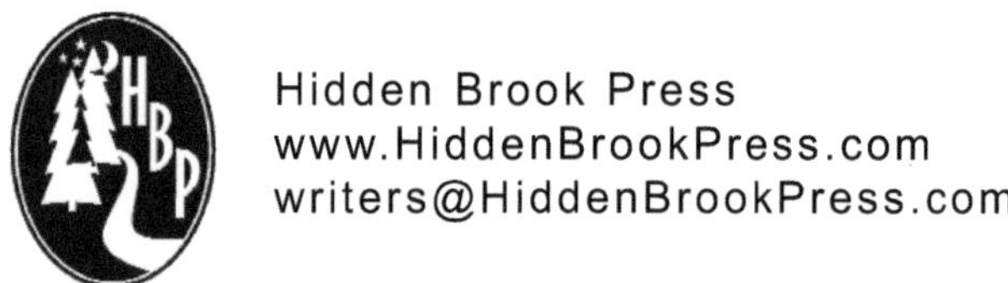

Hidden Brook Press
www.HiddenBrookPress.com
writers@HiddenBrookPress.com

North of Belleville
Haiku by James Deahl
Photography by Richard M. Grove

Layout and Design – Richard M. Grove
Cover Design – Richard M. Grove
Front and BackCover Photographs – Richard M. Grove

Printed and bound in USA

Library and Archives Canada Cataloguing in Publication

Deahl, James, 1945-
     North of Belleville : haiku / James Deahl ; photography,
Richard M. Grove.

ISBN 978-1-897475-79-9

     1. Haiku, Canadian (English). 2. Hastings (Ont. : County)--
Poetry. 3. Wellington (Ont. : County)--Poetry. 4. Hastings
(Ont. : County)--Pictorial works. 5. Wellington (Ont. : County)--
Pictorial works. I. Grove, Richard M. (Richard Marvin), 1953-
II. Title.

PS8557.E223N67 2011   C811'.54   C2011-908736-7

Several of the haiku in this volume were first published in the following magazines; *Icon*, *Mayfly*, *Parmassus Literary Journal* and *RAW NerVZ HAIKU*.

Table of Contents

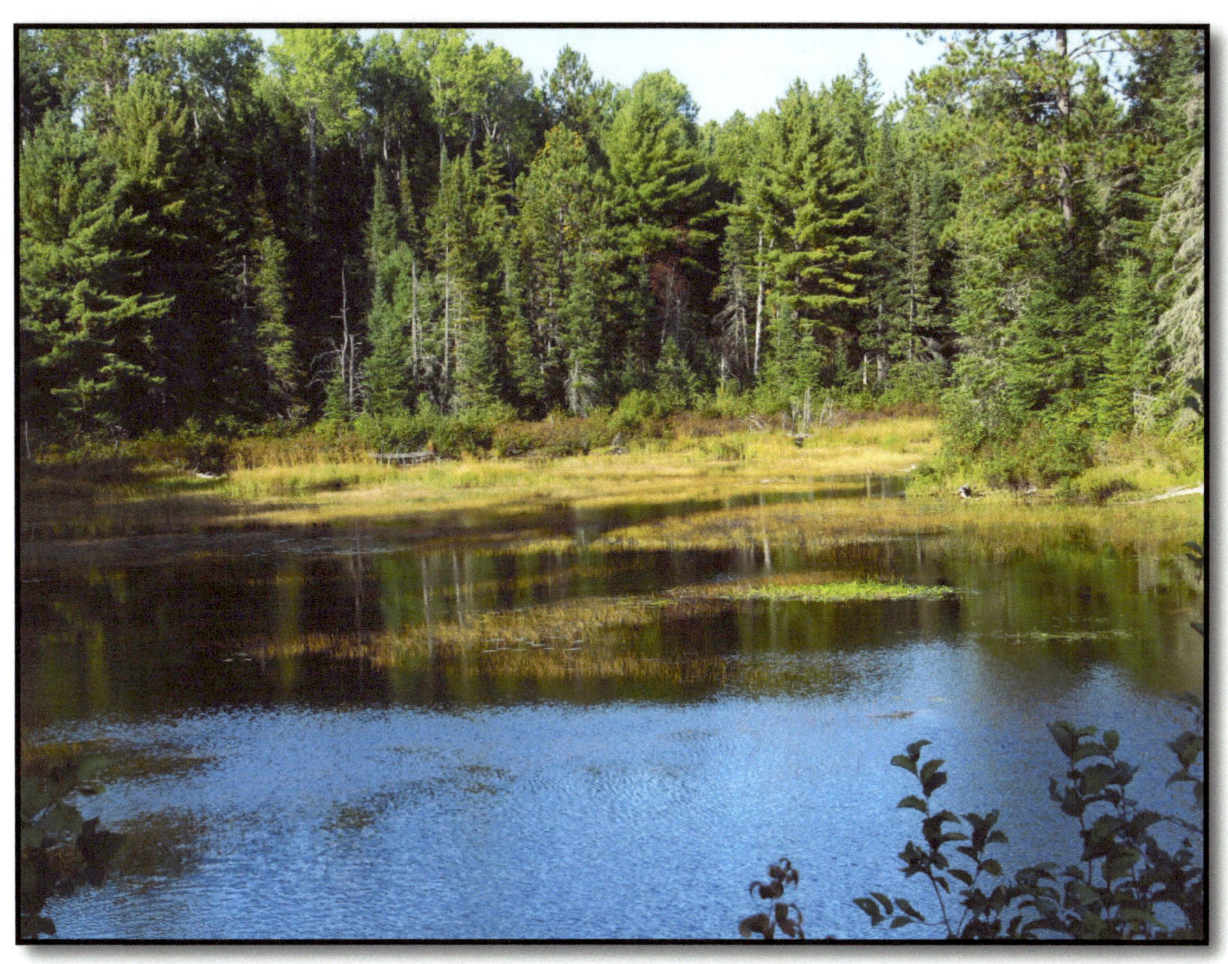

Methodist Graveyard

for Michael Dudley

Not a cloud in sight;
  a red-tailed hawk circles
the shallow valley.

Deep crabgrass —
silent gravestones lean
against a pale sky.

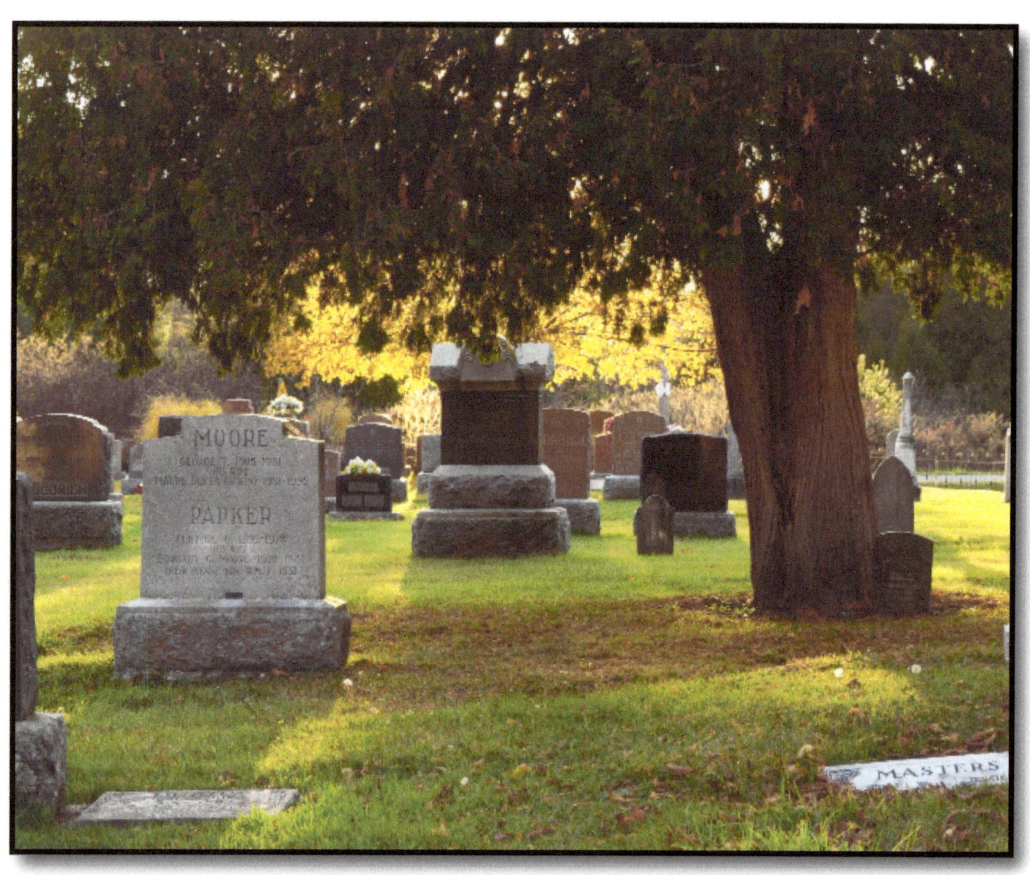

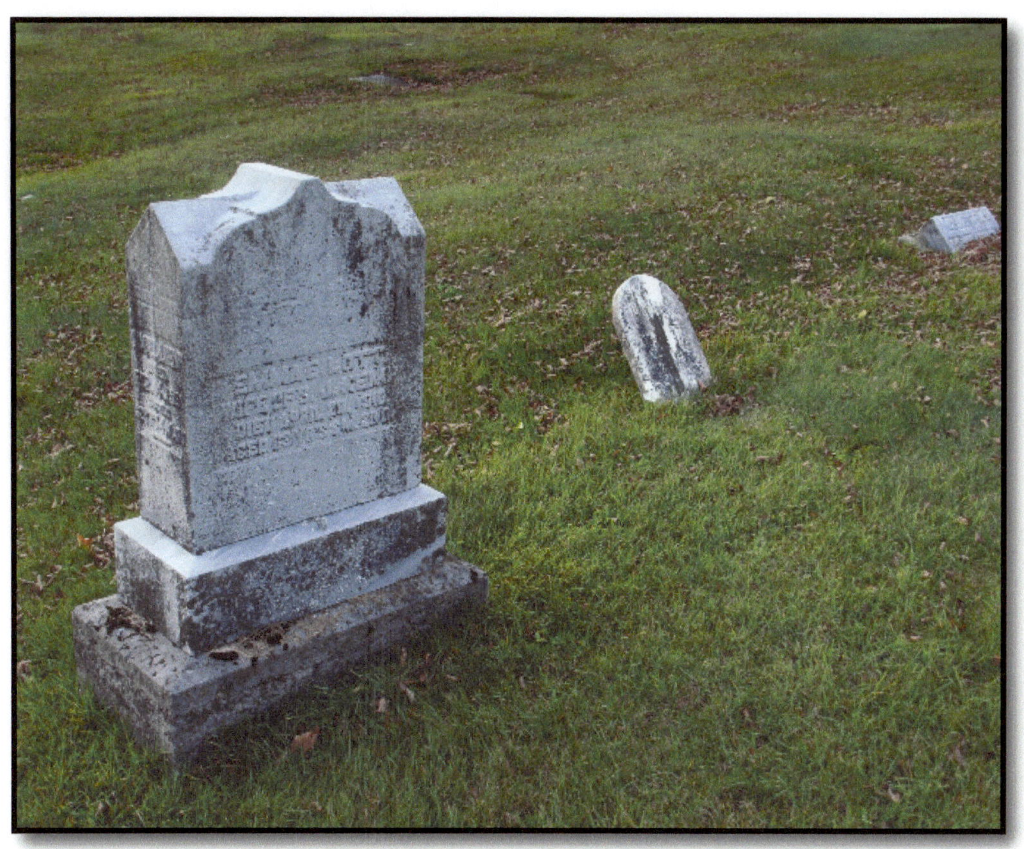

No burials this century,
     silver birch grow wild
the untended plot.

   Two pheasants burst
from behind a broken marker —
   morning stillness.

   Hawk at daybreak —
the strong, curved beak skinning
   a strayed cat.

Steel Valley

The steeltown —
    smoke from blast furnaces
first time in years.

    Charging red furnaces —
the steel mill surrounded
    by spring willows.

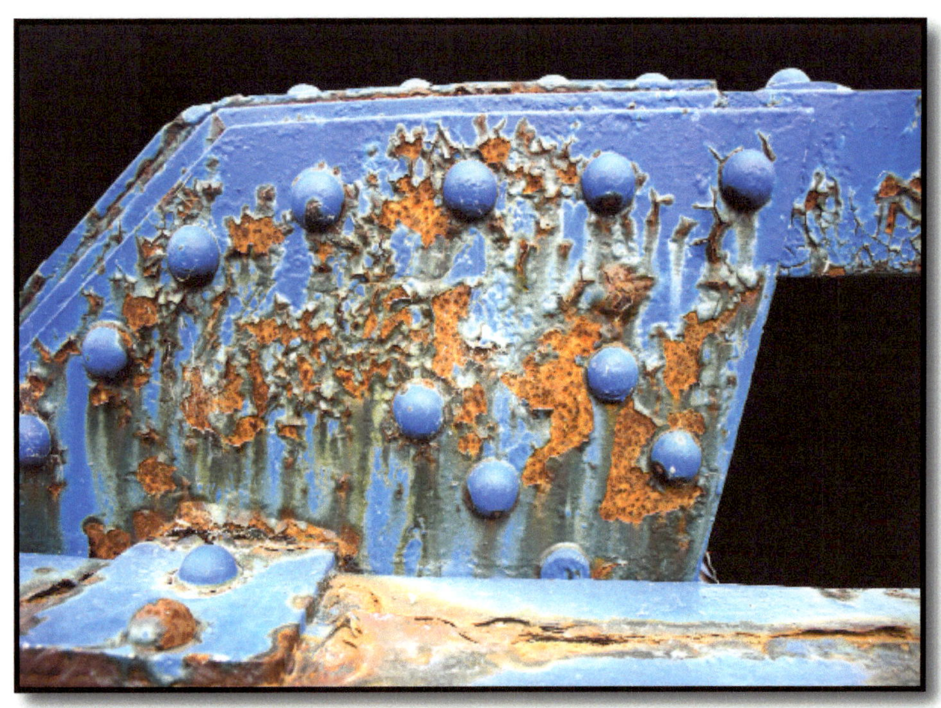

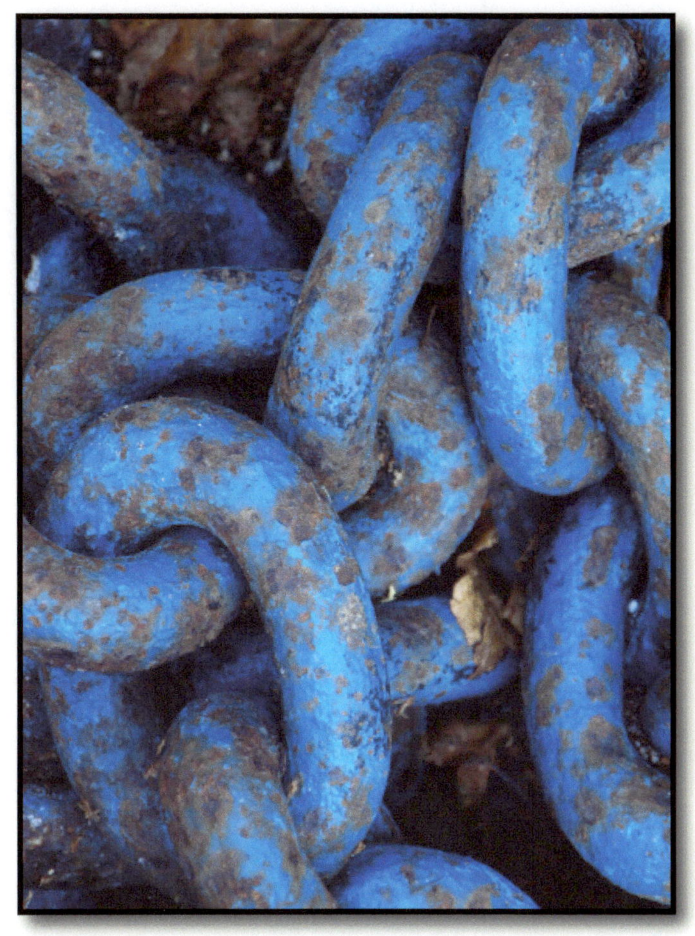

First thaw —
    fields of clotted mud,
old boilerhouse.

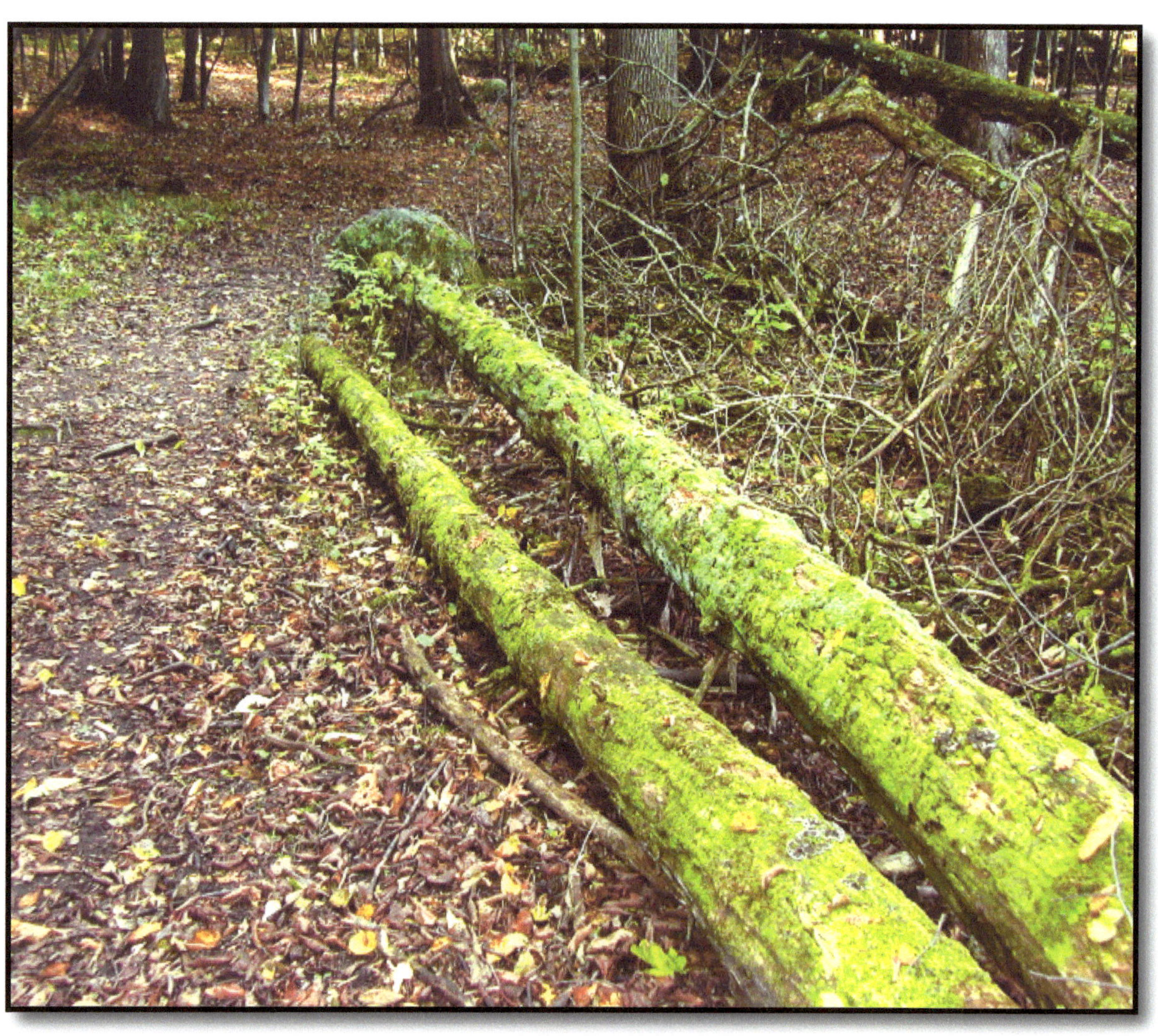

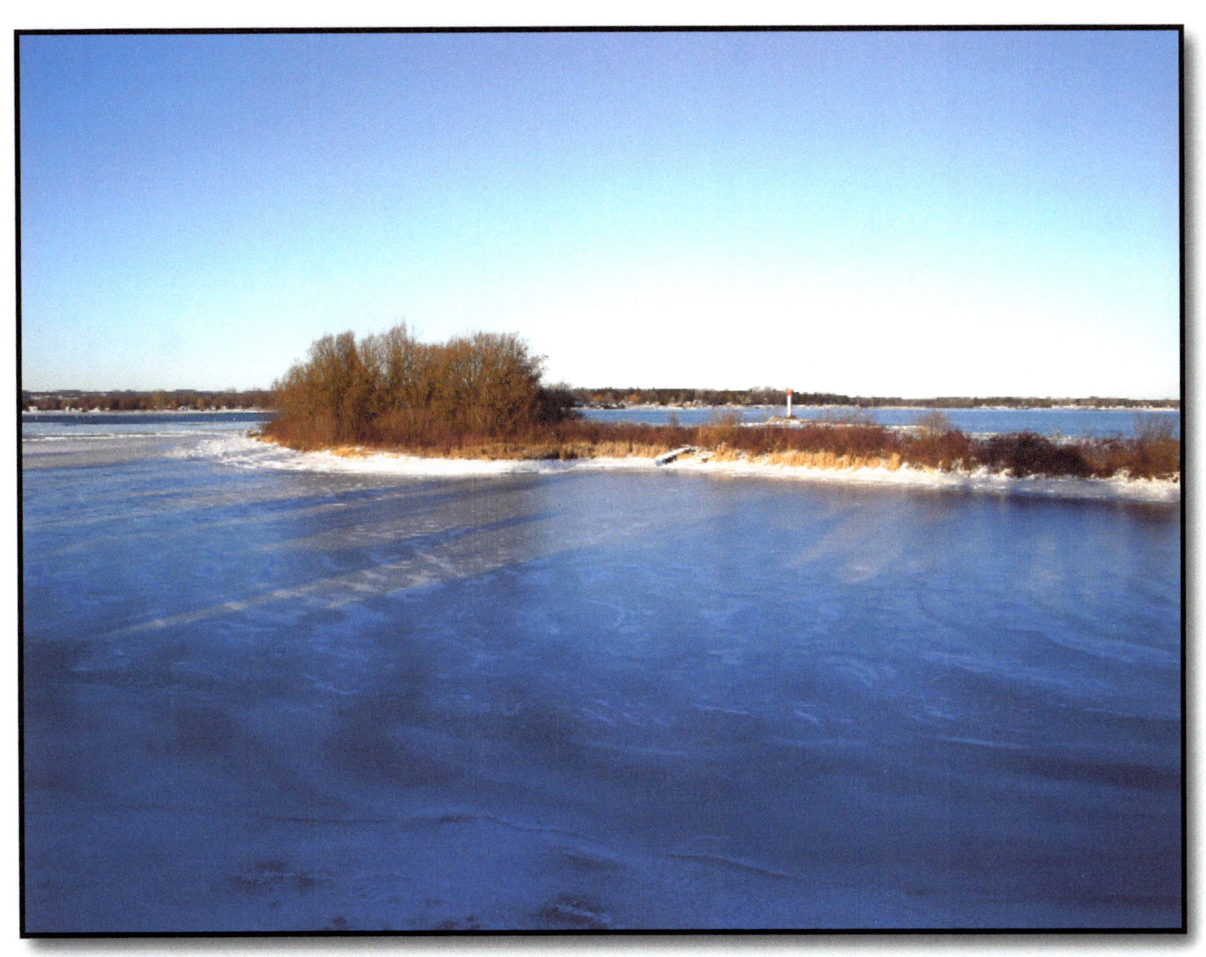

Red Hill Valley

Under storm clouds
   the voice of Albion Falls —
cold as ice.

Deep in King's Forest
   the creek lies buried
      in yellow leaves.

   October valley —
one spruce set green against
   frost-red maples.

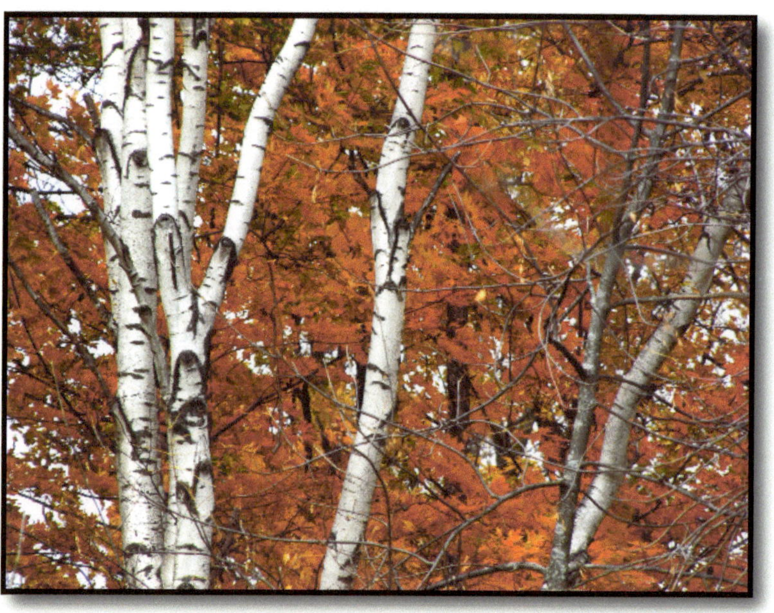

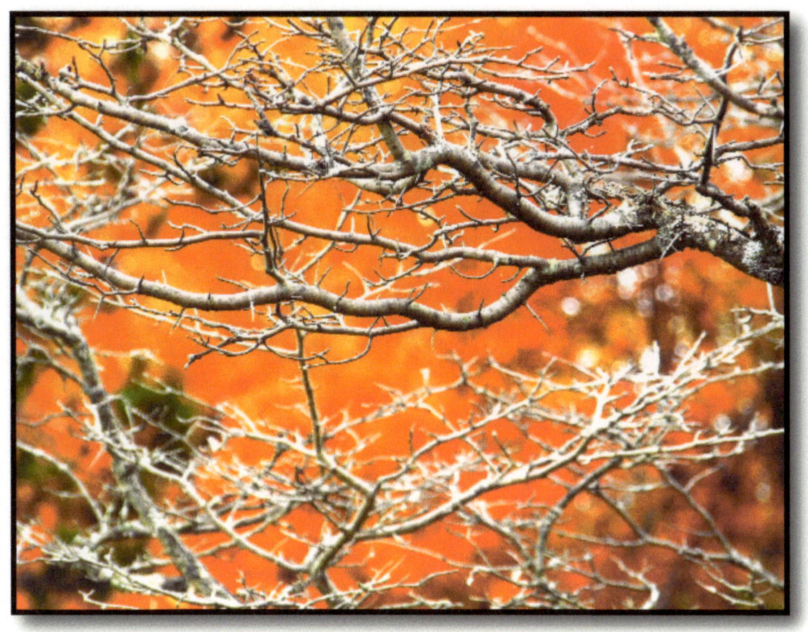

Almost like rain
the sound of leaves falling
    in autumn wind.

Far northern woods —
hemlocks growing straight from rock
   recall my home.

Two brooks join —
maples raise flaming hands
   to an empty sky.

Clutched by the roots
    of a storm-downed elm
the fossil.

At the headwaters
this season's cattails weep
for their fallen brothers.

Deep in the valley
   only a few white asters
      welcome the cold season.

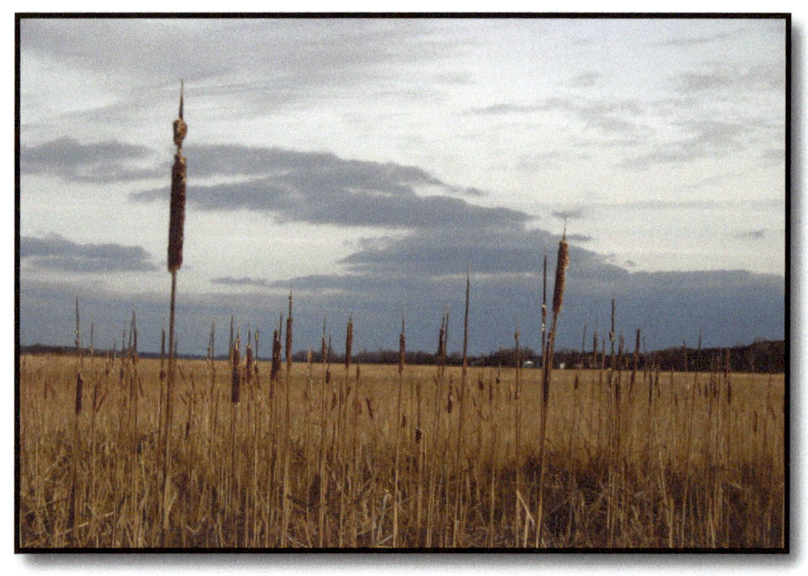

Last week autumn,
today the first bare trees
    summon the north wind.

Like praying monks
    overlooking the stream
these blackened sumacs.

Intricate nest
of storm-spun hawthorn branches
revealed by one cold wind.

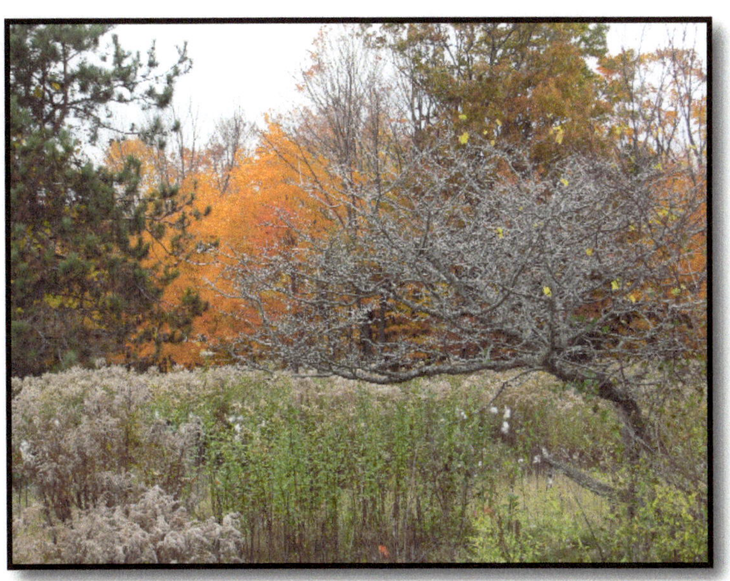

Even in death
the withered teasel
still frightens.

The sumac's red blaze
    cannot warn my cold spirit
        as winter nears.

Hornets visit
    this field of goldenrod
        one last time.

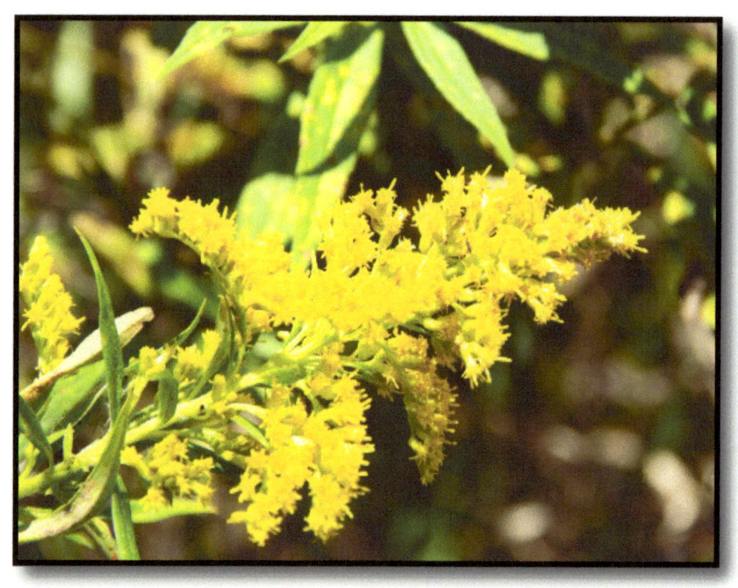

Mountain pine —
its lower branches overrun
   by yellowed grapevines.

   Unable to flee
these trees will soon parish
   beneath the wild grape.

   Once farmland
now sumac and raspberries
   unlock the earth.

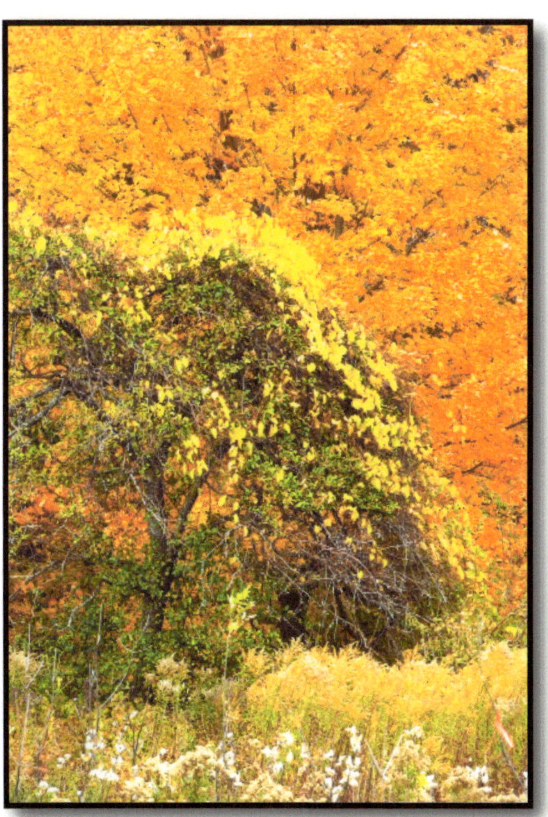

So far from roads —
car tire embedded
   in a dry creek bed.

Red cliffs at sunset —
sugar maples overlean
   scarlet water.

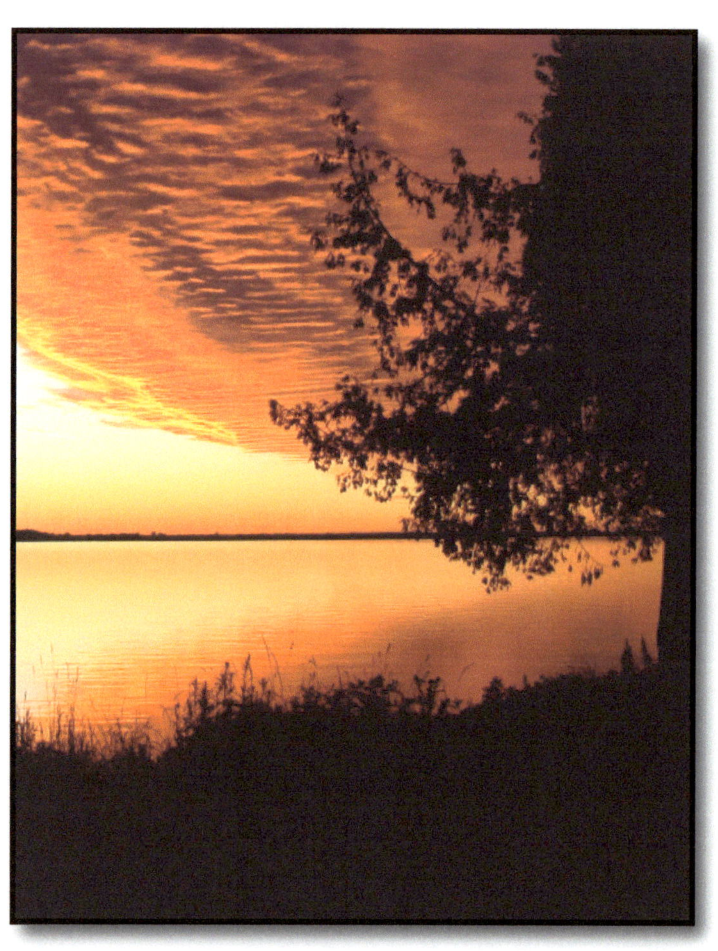

Grove of dead trees —
crickets welcome
    the autumn night.

Rafts of leaves
    float downstream
still, minnows remain.

Completely still
the creek at dusk
    opens its dark heart.

A campfire's flame
    pierces the darkness
        crickets have brought.

No one walks this trail —
the silence
    I share with insects.

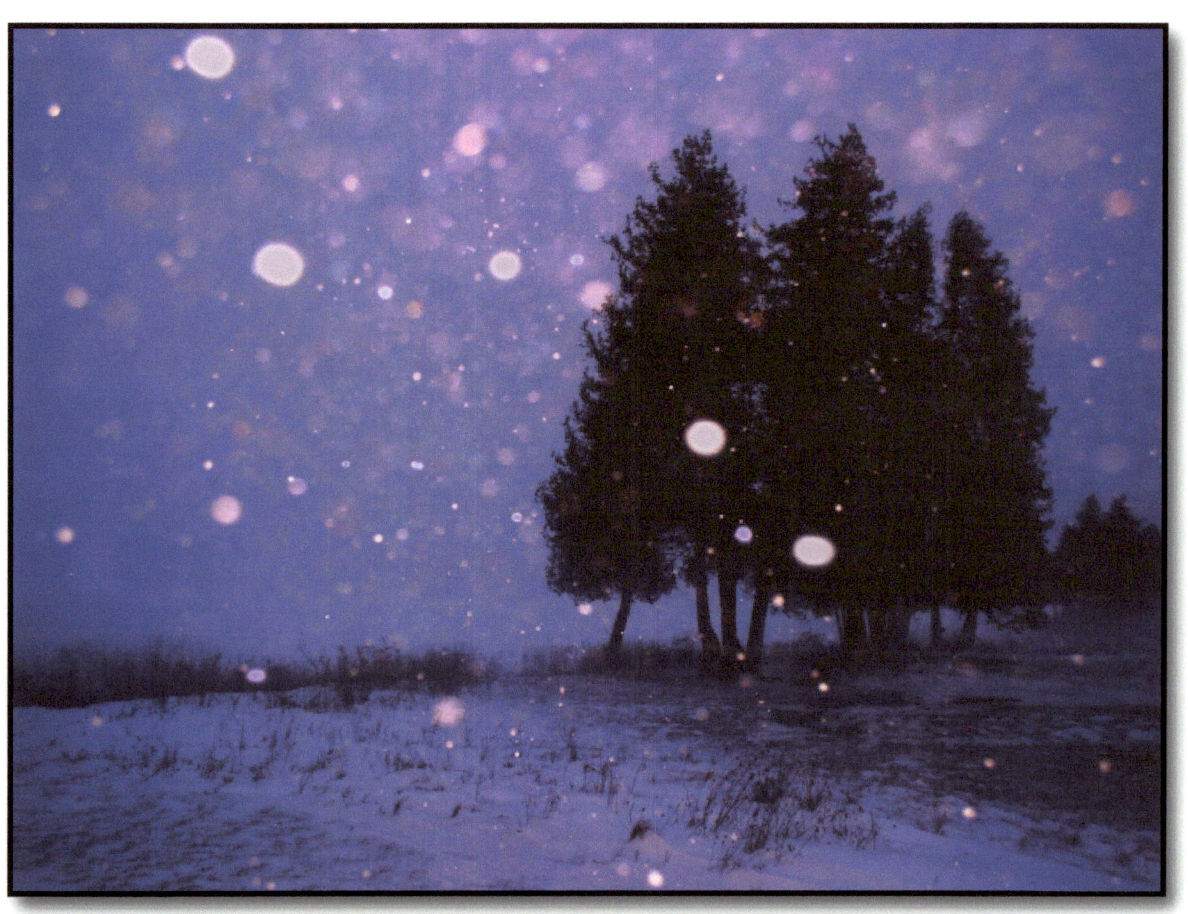

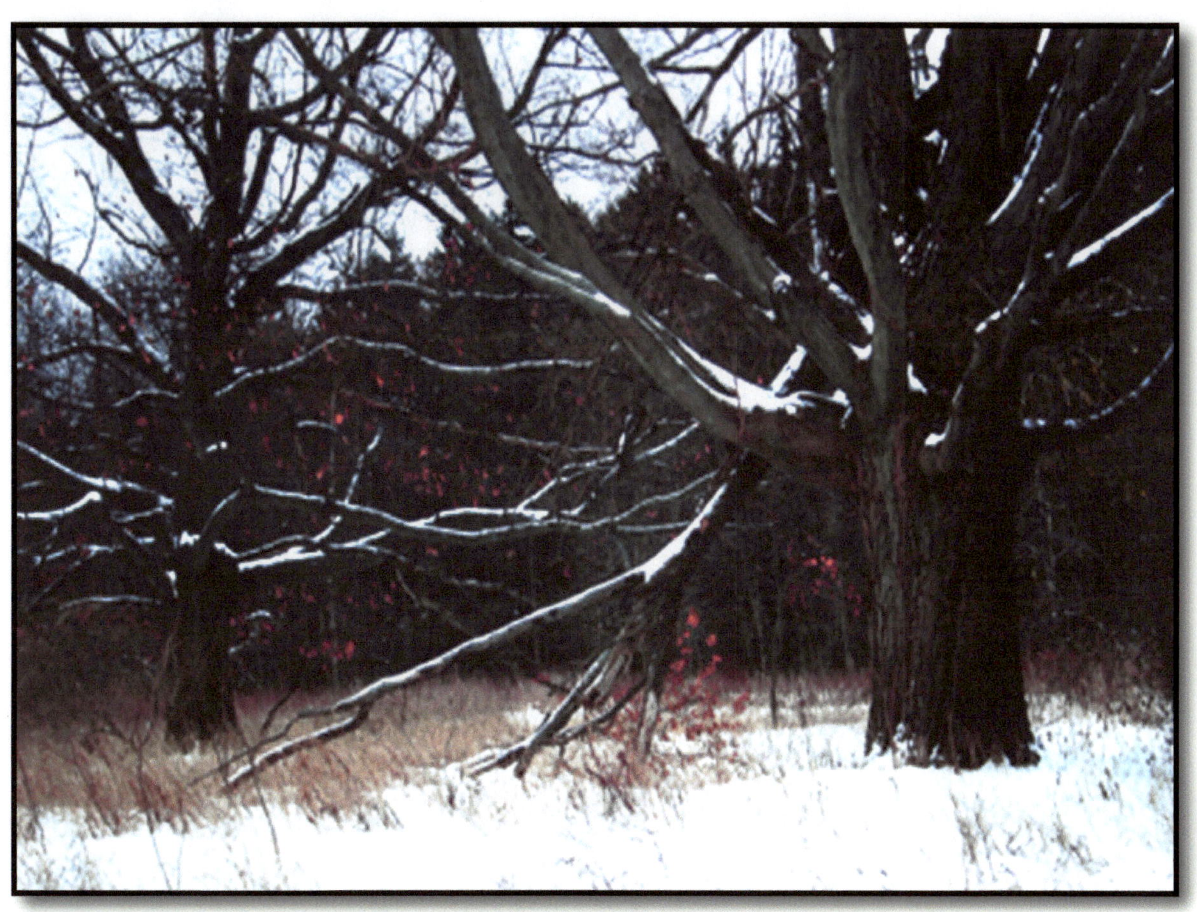

At Bald Eagle Camp

Spider's web
  thirty feet up in hemlock
ensnared in white dew.

Shallow mountain brook
and the roar of motorcycles
penetrate the dark laurel.

Deep in the north country
  this single mossy brick
worn by the stream.

Pre-dawn cold —
around a long dead beech
mountain laurel in bloom.

  Looking for firewood;
a stag's skull hidden
  among red flowers.

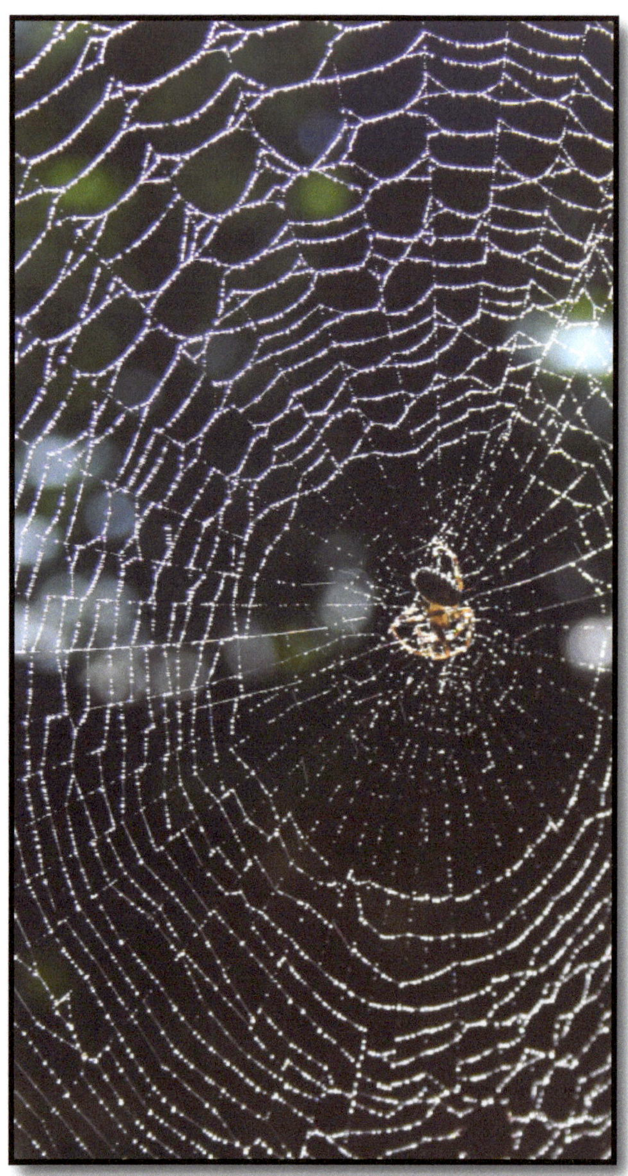

McMaster Trail

The maple so dense
not a fleck of sunlight
even at noon.

The sun's too hot —
mosquitoes and I share
a linden's shade.

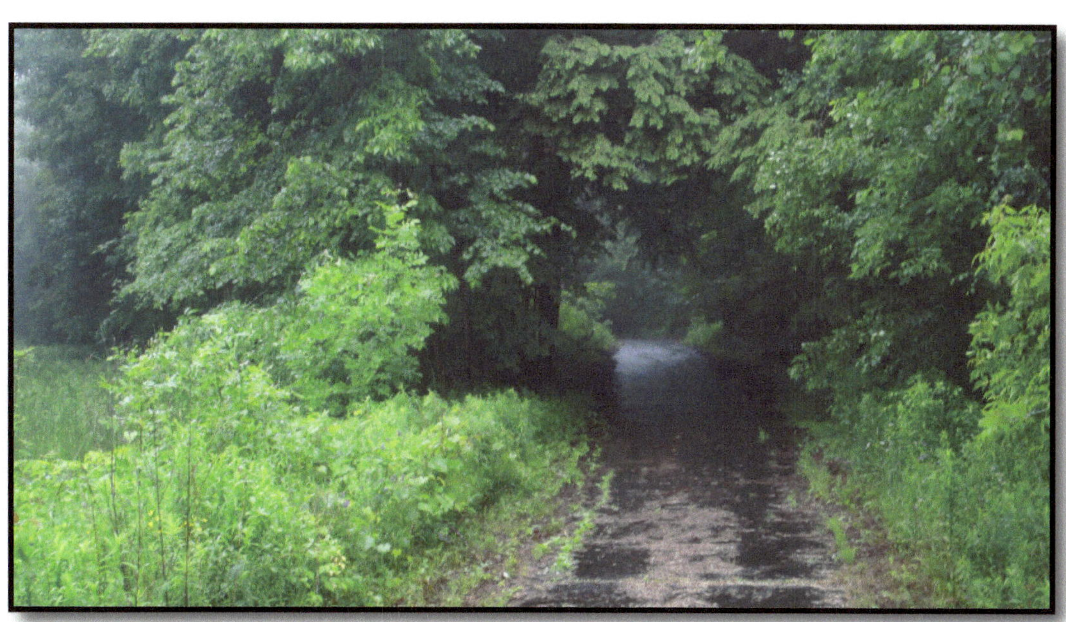

The spring moon
   held in the black lake,
      in the windless trees.

    A red-wing's cry —
fragrance of sage and basil
   escapes the garden.

Afternoon closes —
from every shadowed thicket
  bird cries shape the dark.

Even on Sunday
  gardens must be hoed and watered —
day of no rest.

The old man
  at the end of his bean row
    straightens gnarled fingers.

Where the farmhouse stood
  two tulips amid jewelweed
remember.

  Wild irises —
the afternoon silence
  stained purple.

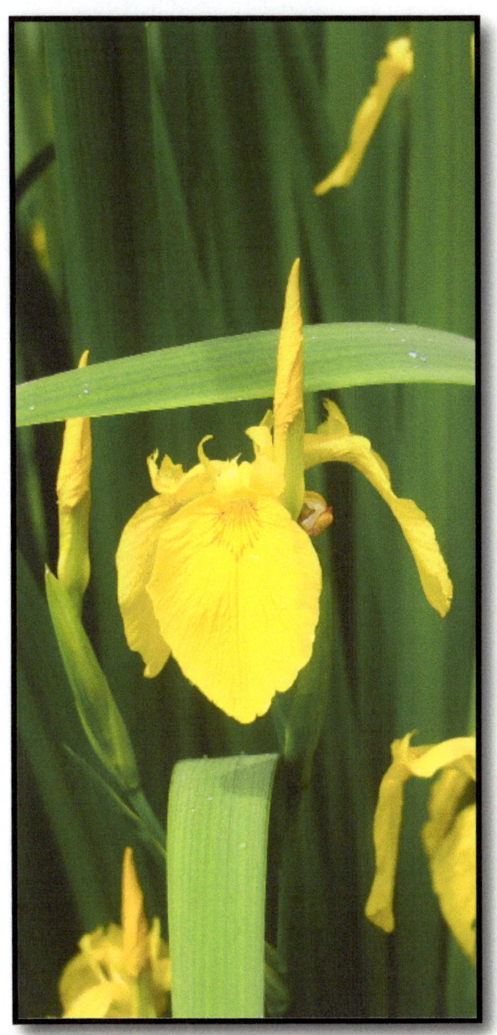

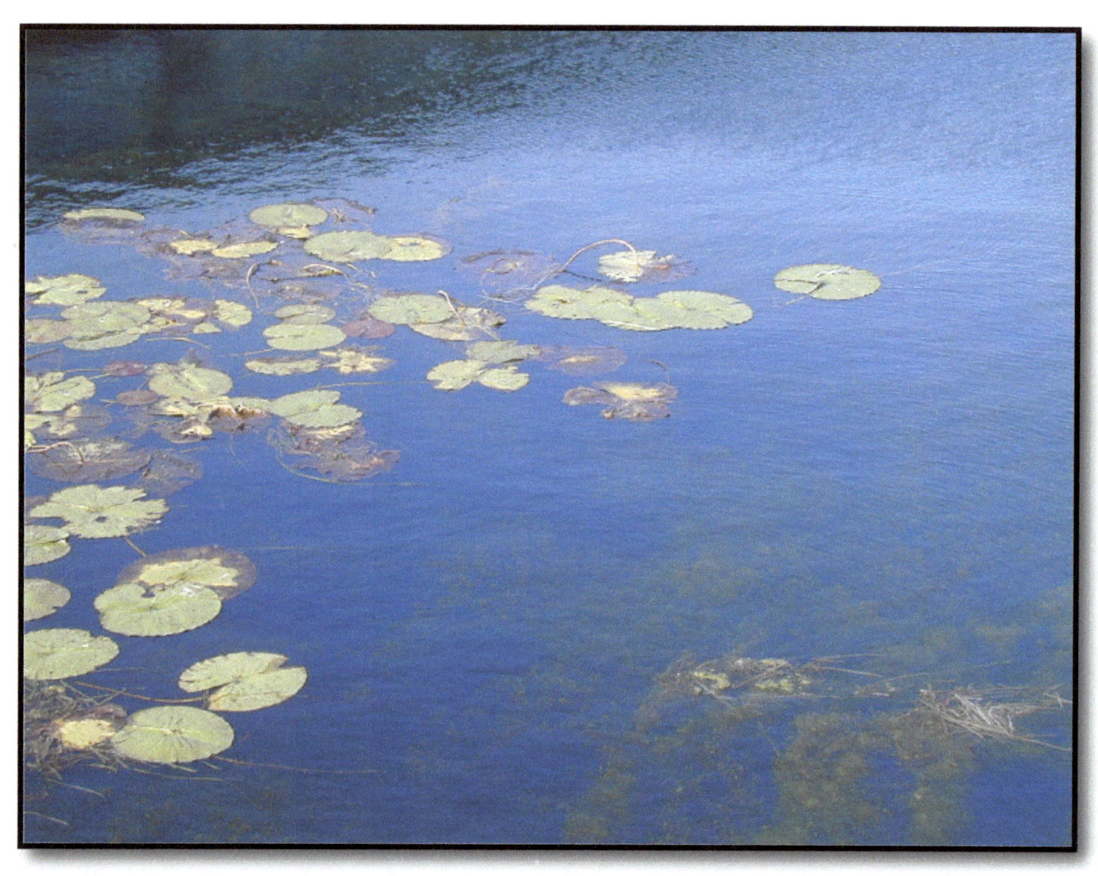

Spring night —
how deep the sky
over this pond.

Sassafras Point

Only May —
peonies, roses
in full bloom.

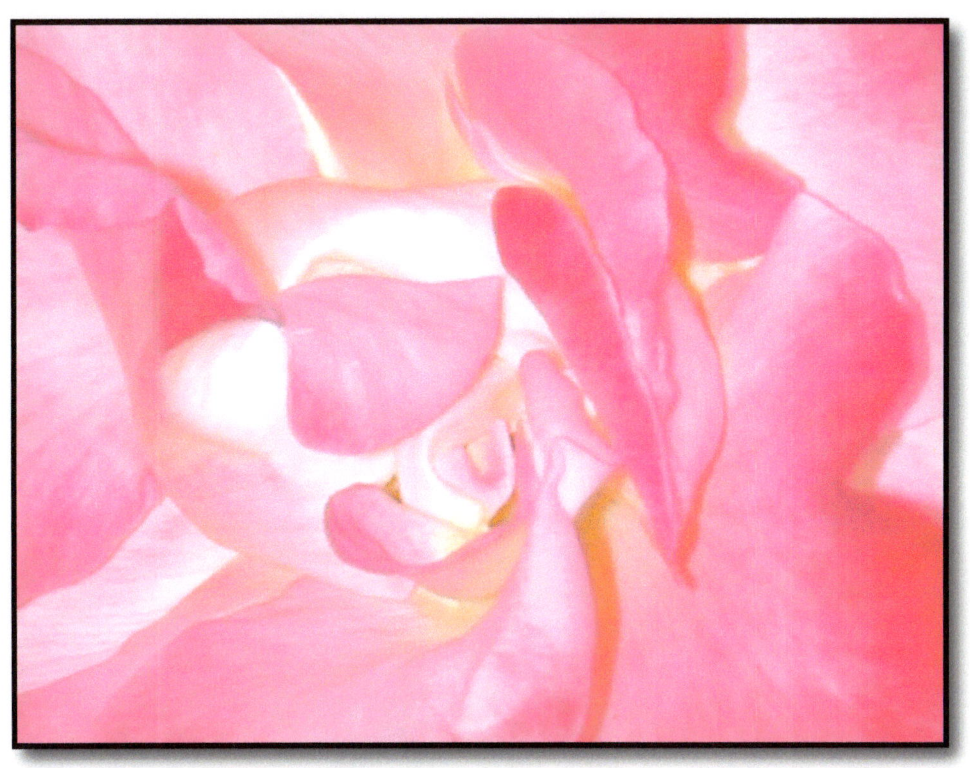

Wild mallow —
sassafras saplings cast
their net of shadows.

The whole tree
stripped clear
by inchworms.

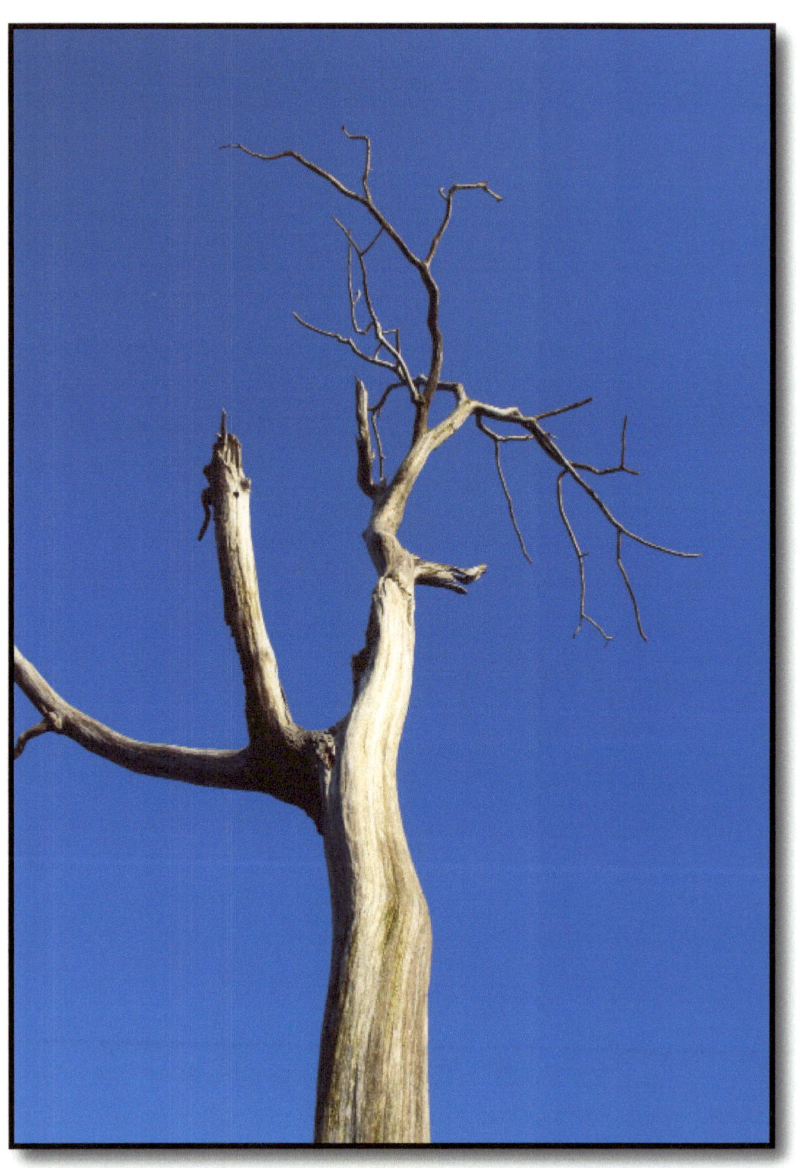

The distant train —
red cars vanish one by one
    amid spring trees.

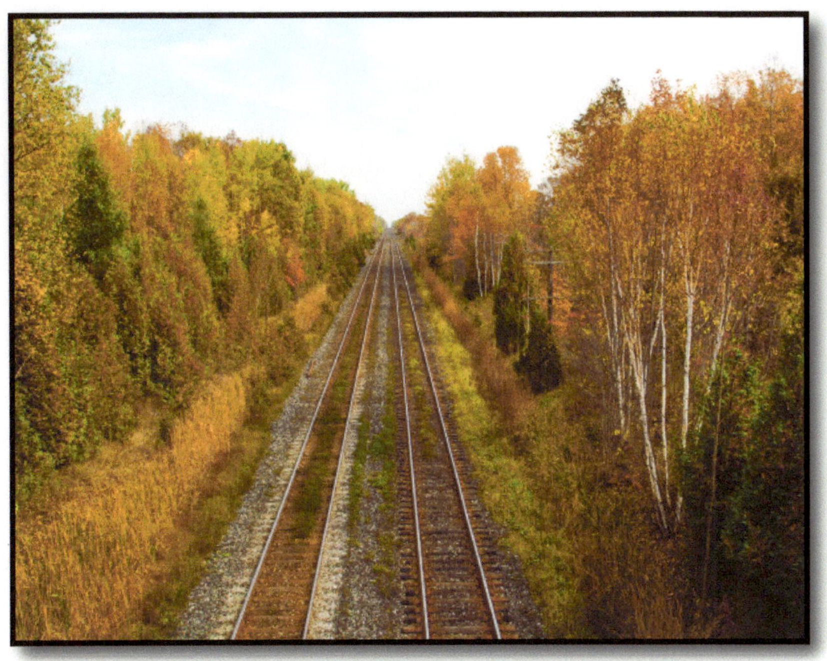

Lovers share a canoe
their strokes perfected
        by habit.

The willow struck
    by last autumn's lightning —
still alive.

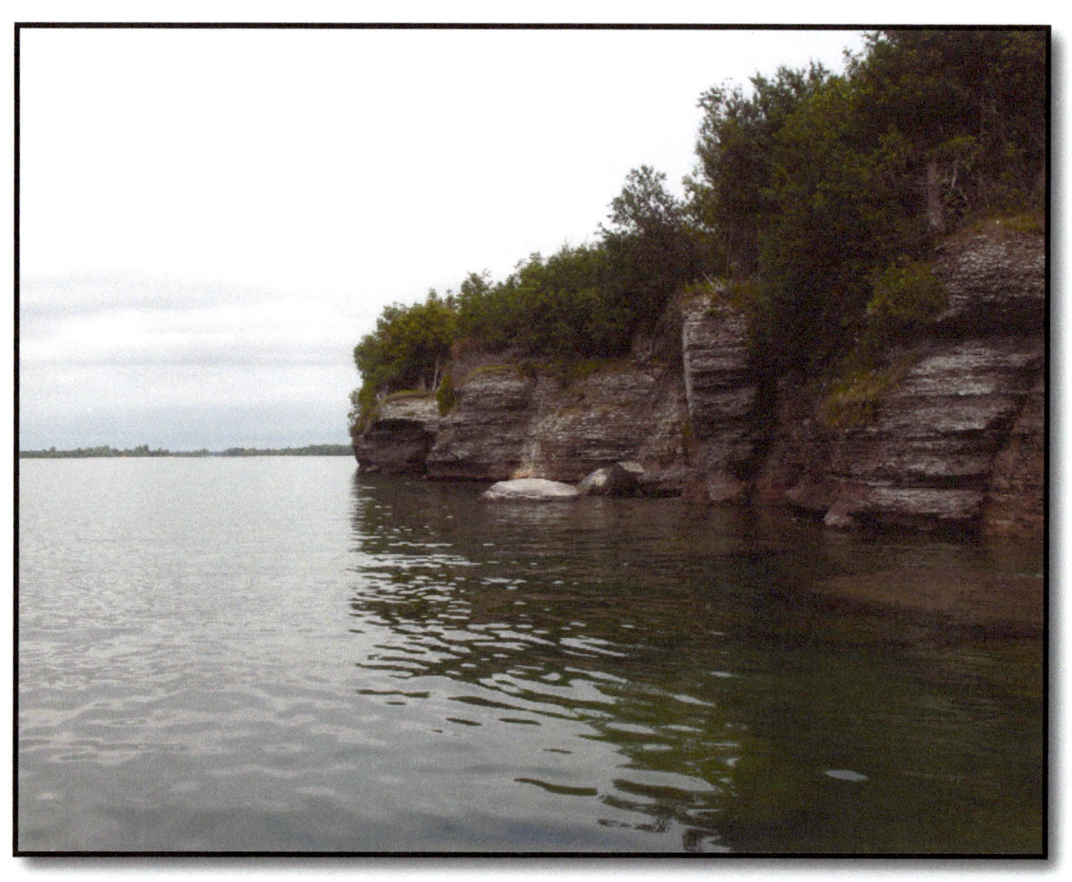

So far from town
a single columbine overlooks
this empty bay.

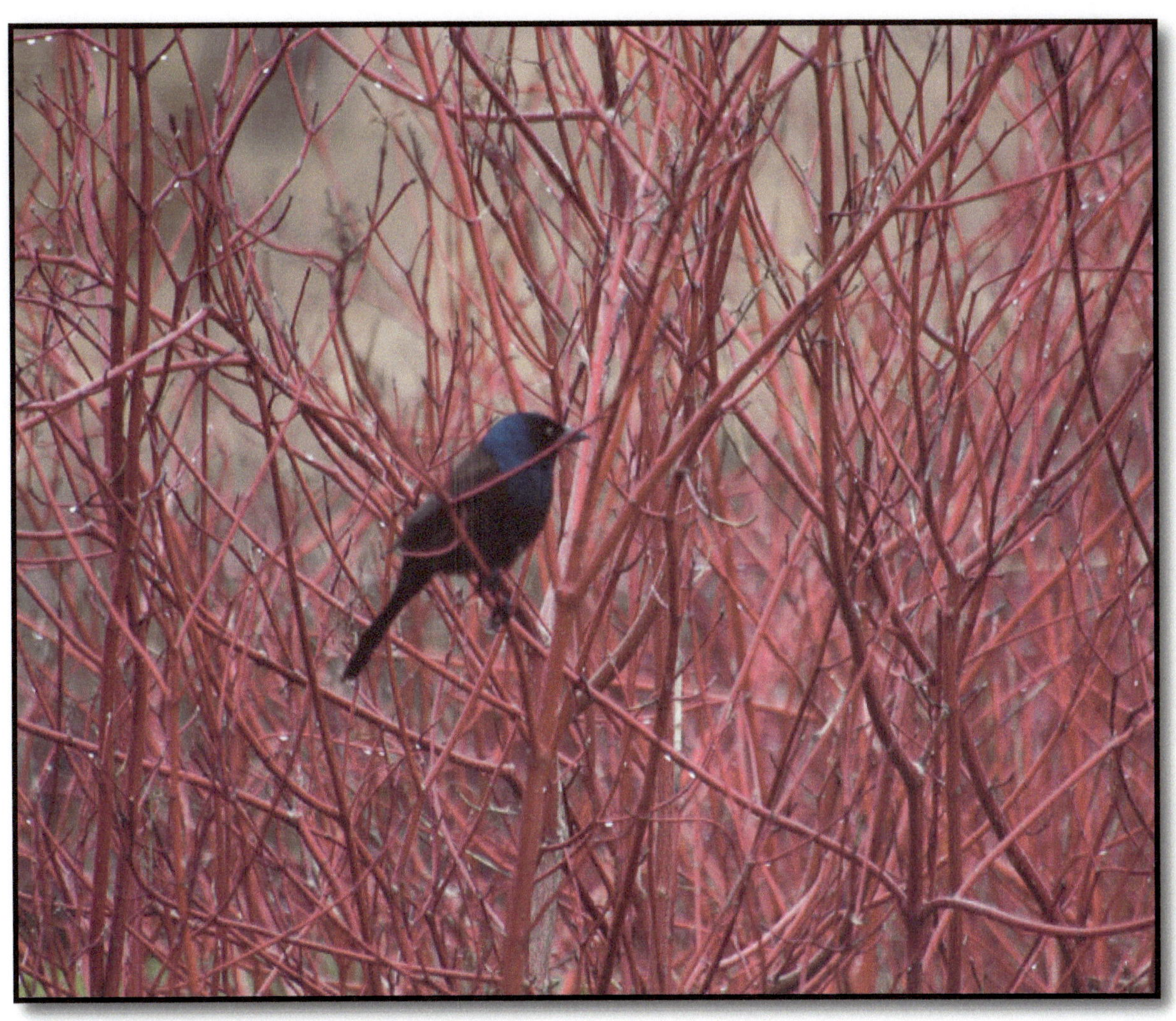

Wellington County Spring

Skies clear —
along river shadows
a heron fishes.

Maple flowers
stain the dark pavement
April red.

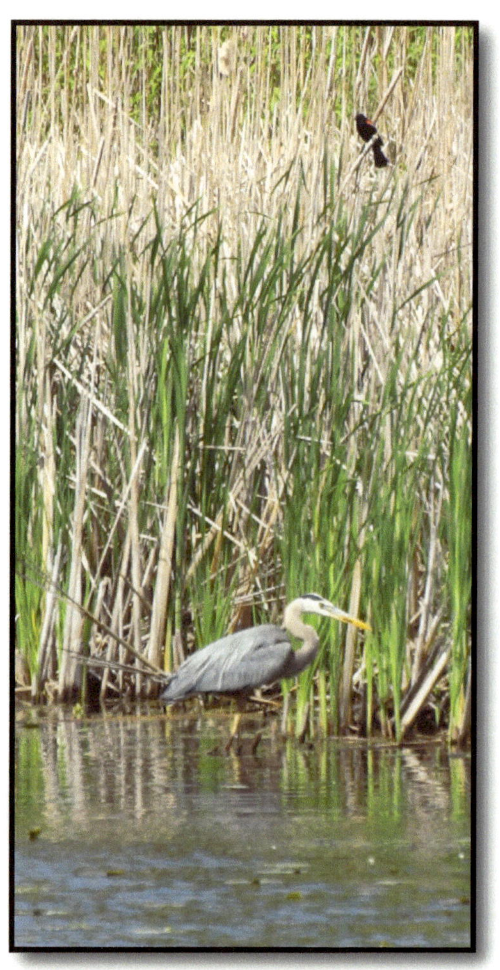

Spanning the river
the bridge trembles beneath
hard iron wheels.

From the valley's heart
the song of water
between dark banks.

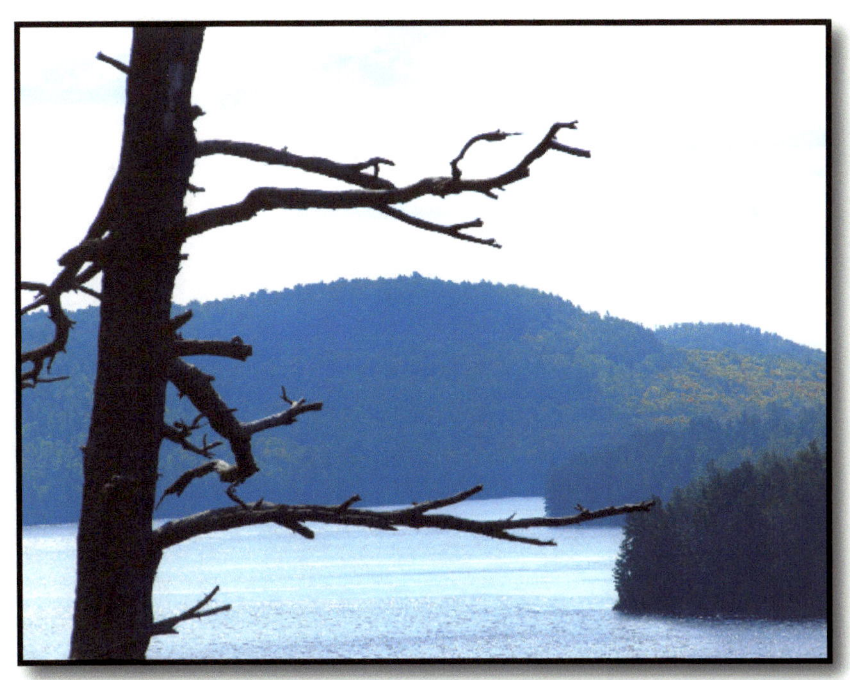

Without effort
the muskrat dives,
becomes ripples.

Fields left fallow
I sense last autumn's corn
as dusk gathers.

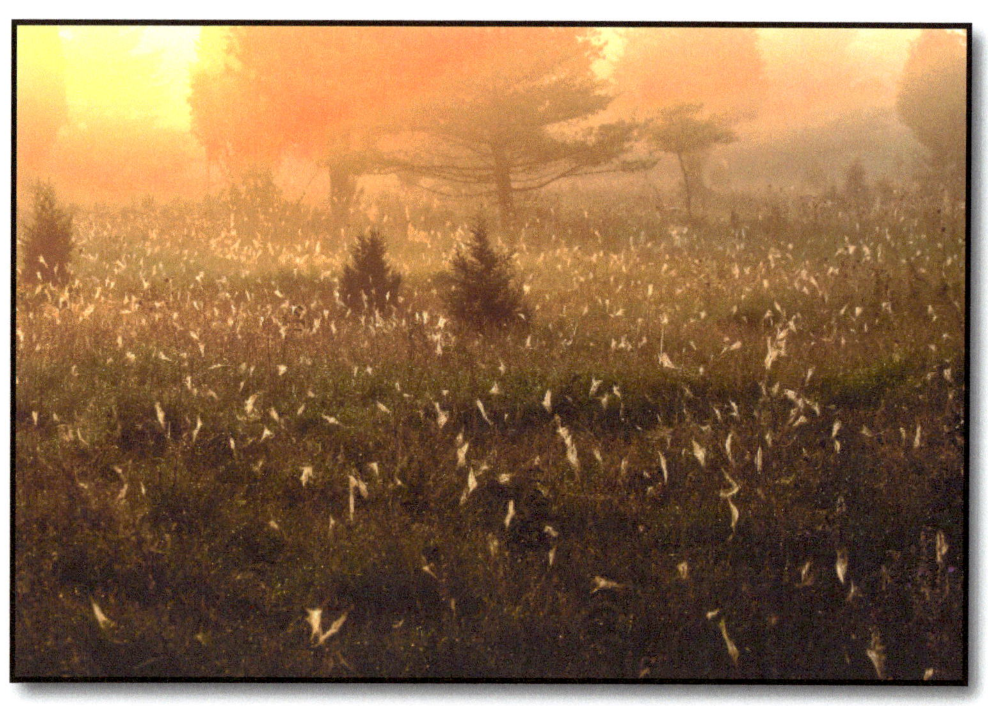

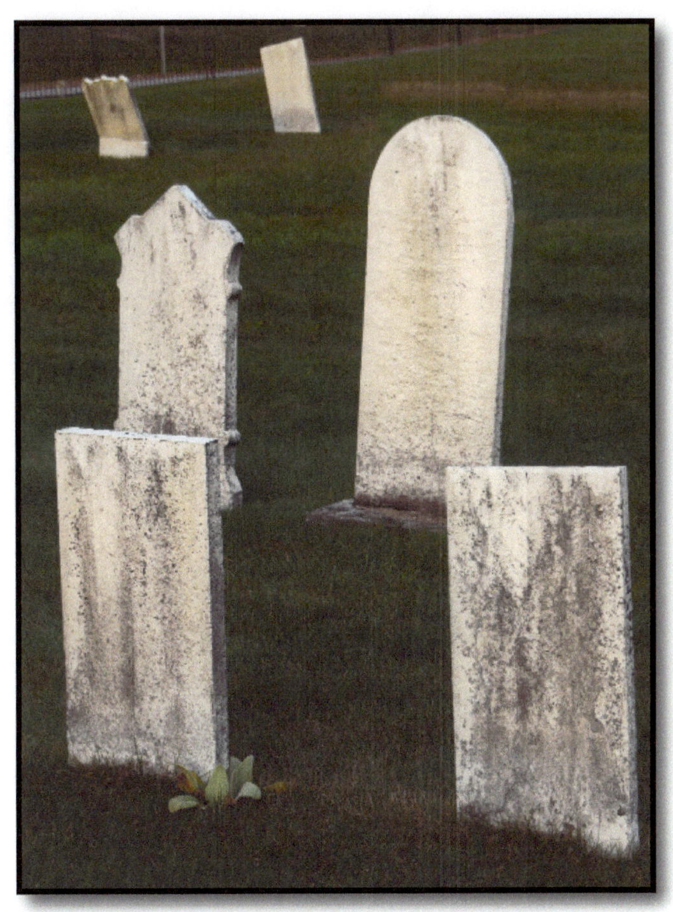

Among bleached stems
slim green shoots welcome
the returning sun.

As rain clouds gather:
a field of dead Germans
in the chapel's shadow.

I walk slowly
listening to wind in a spruce
    roving free.

Fieldstone house —
martins nest
under dark eves.

Pale sky —
    trees rise
from the opened fields.

The road stretches west;
    we journey
        through endless pastures.

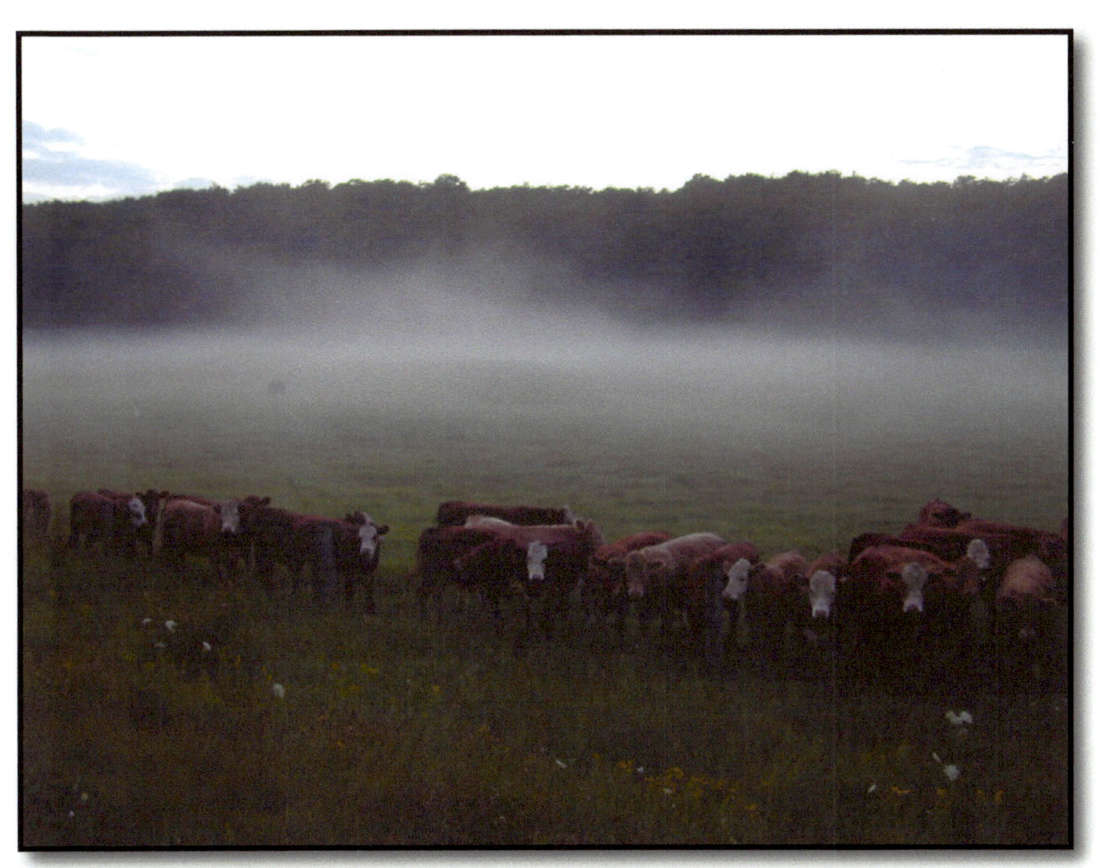

Hidden nest —
with fanned tail
the male killdeer challenges us.

Carp feed
among reflected branches
of bare trees.

Setting sun —
   in every man's shadow
a silence.

At sunrise
birds skim the furrows
for insects.

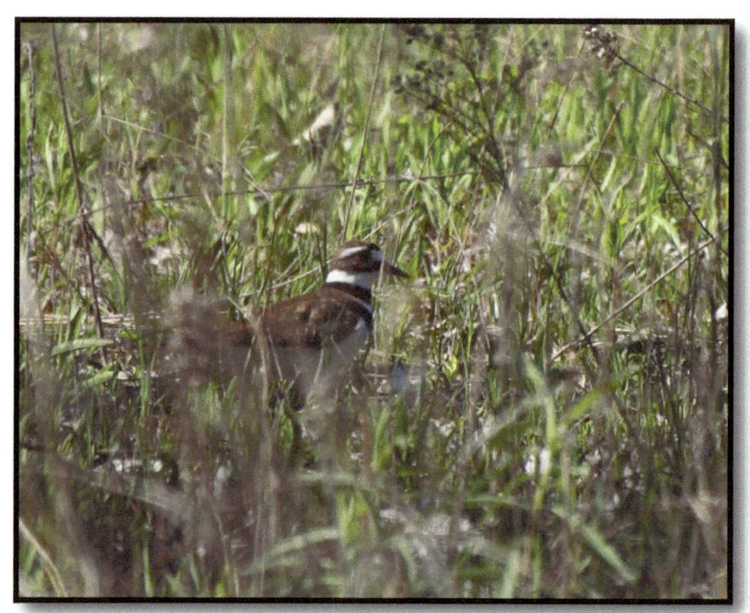

From every side
the slice of ploughs
through clotted loam.

    Near the creek
bur oaks stand knee-deep
    in their reflections.

In evening's shadows
the ploughed garden
waiting for seeds.

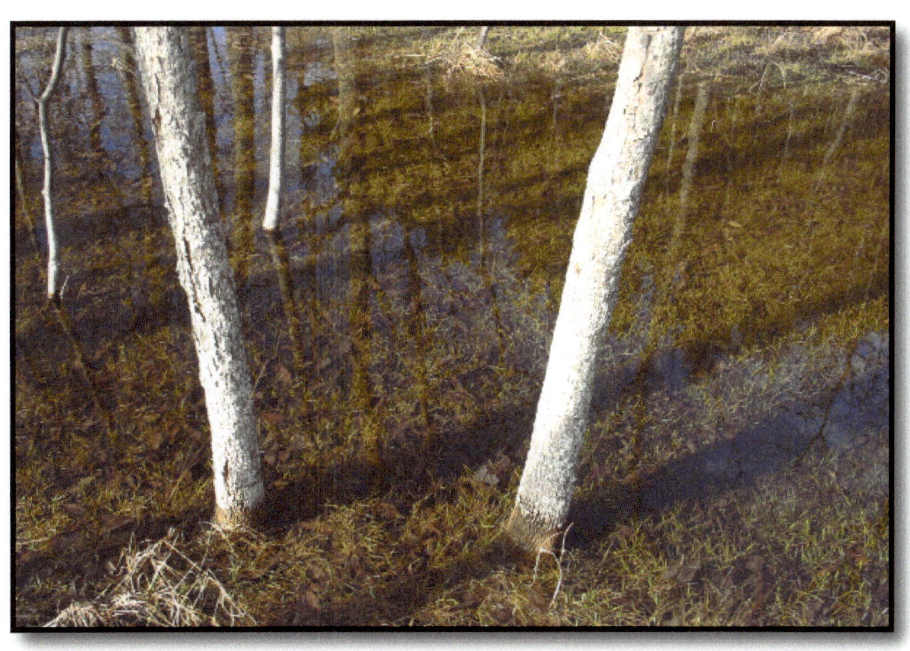

Wellington County Autumn

The hawk's feathers
 ruffled by the first wind
  of autumn.

   At the millrace
shadows of dove and killdeer
 touch cold water.

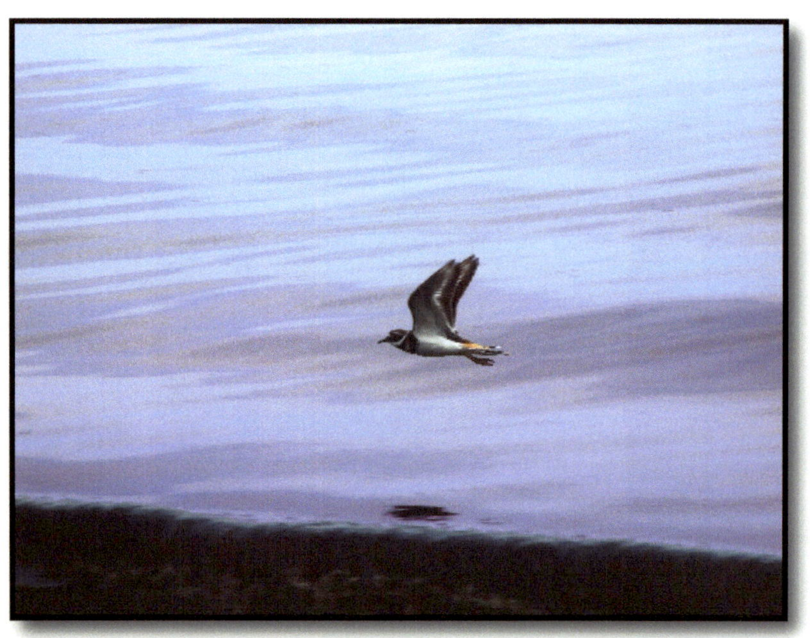

As the rain starts
generator door bangs
     again and again.

Feed corn gone
a white cat zigzags across
     deep furrows.

     Low to the east
Orion obscured
     by black maples.

False dawn —
a rooster's sudden call
pierces the rain.

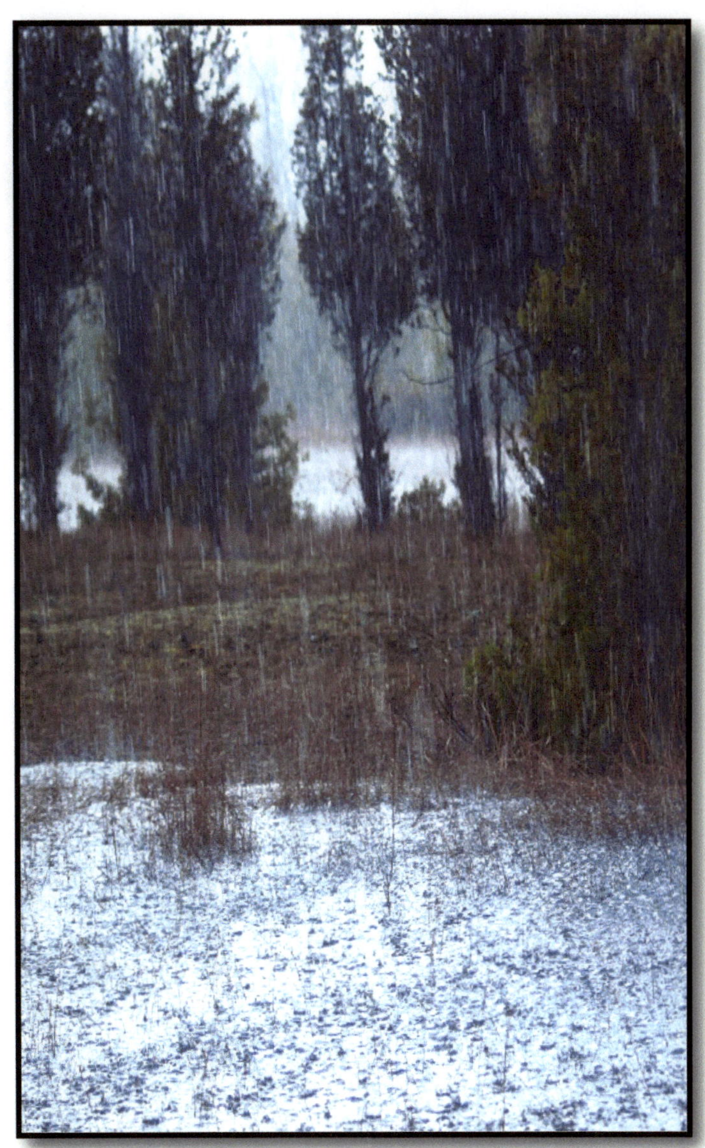

Driving to work
paper birch leaves
on a yellow wind.

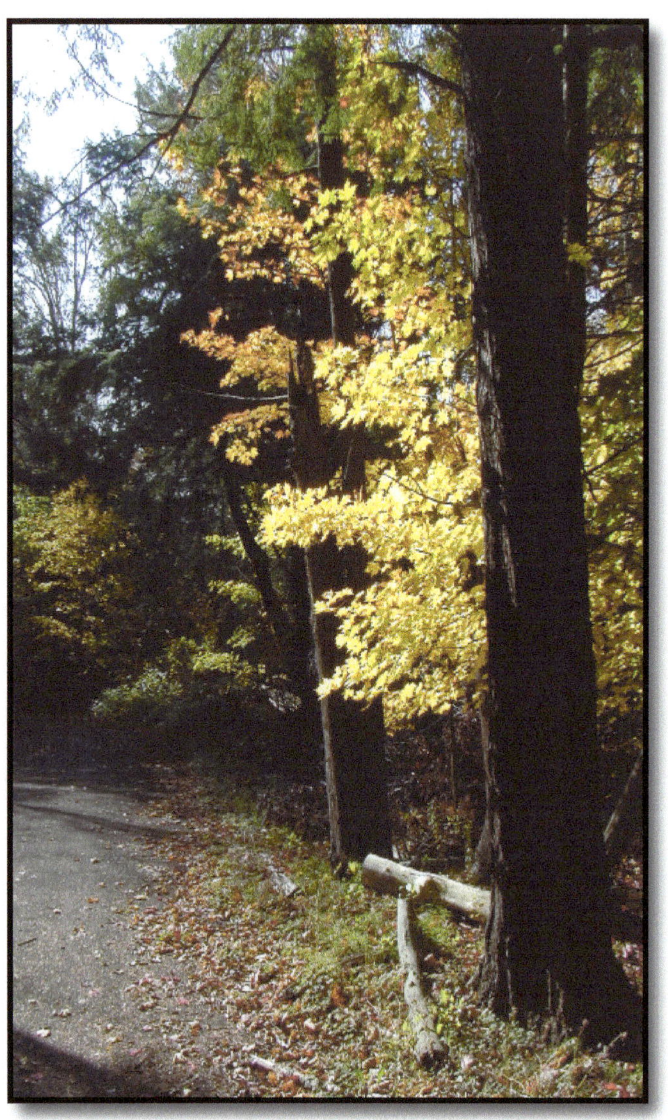

Valley of the Conestogo:
    the river a blue scar
        through cleared fields.

    Creosoted sleepers
piled in weeds
    by an empty station.

    A frog leaps
into night's
    green silence.

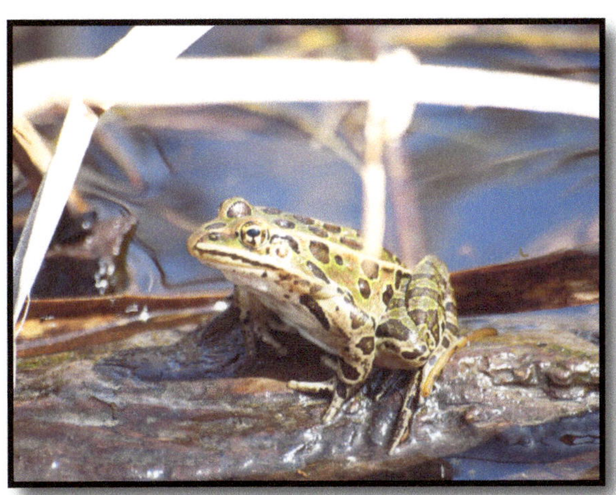

Another night alone —
    stars rise
through torn cloud.

Overhead
    the vault of deep space,
this whole town dark.

Around black trunks
    oak leaves
        bury the grass.

At approaching footsteps
    pigeons burst
from a rusty trestle.

Sound of laughter —
children entering the
municipal library.

Autumn trees
red beyond red
light the sky.

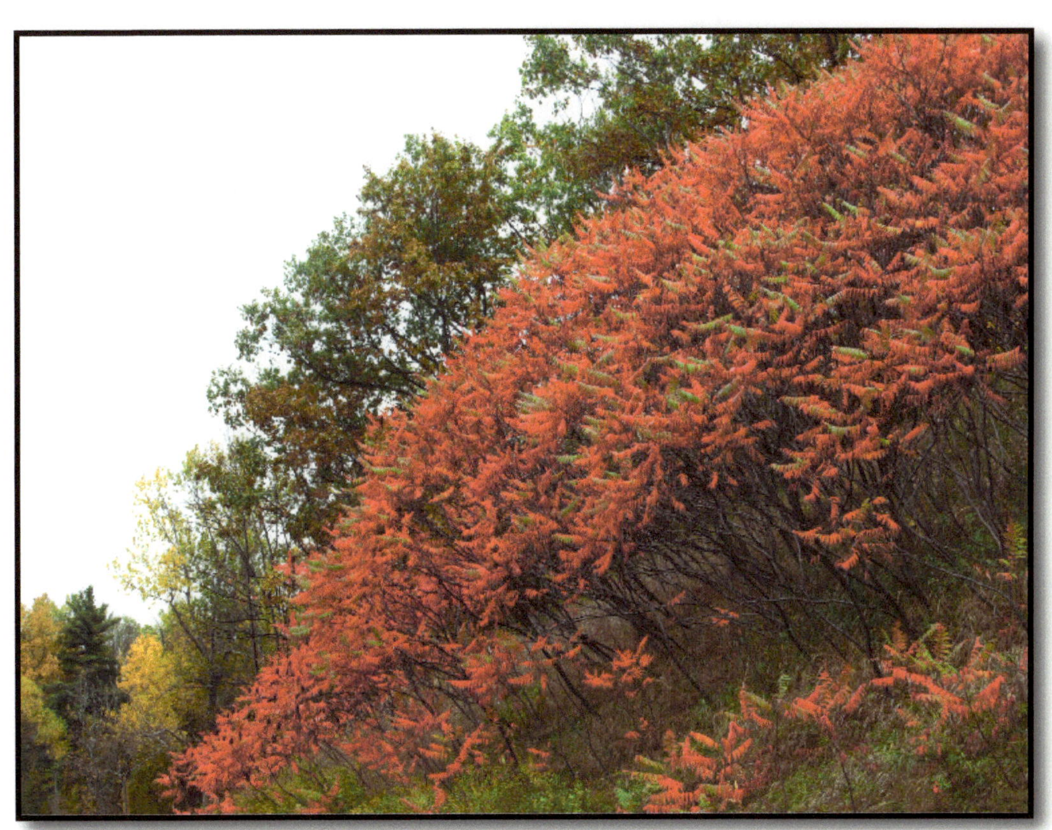

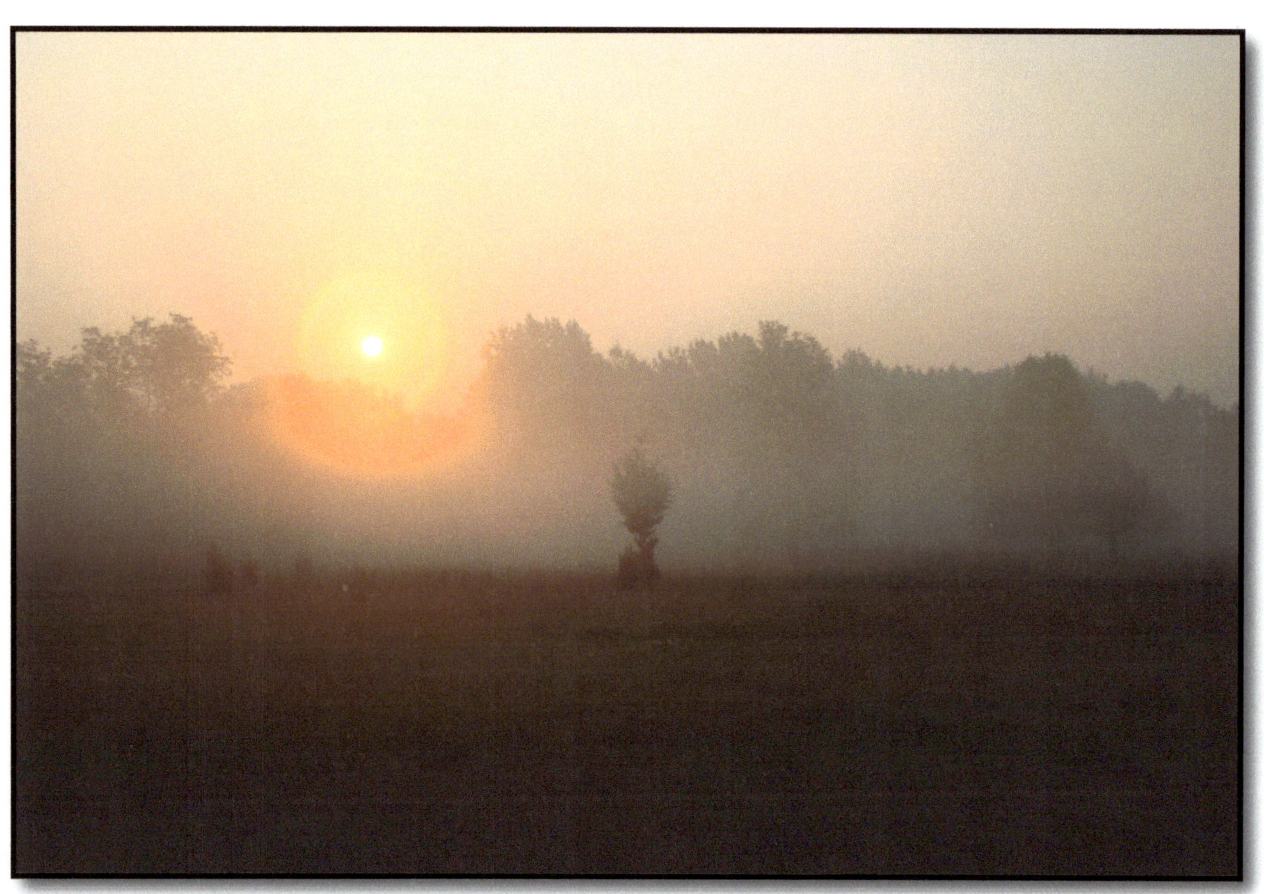

Forty years
          since I entered grade school —
quiet afternoon.

In every heart
     a thorn —
our burden of sorrow.

     Mist and morning flush,
miles of farmland
   at first light.

North Of Belleville

Smoke from a highrise
straight into frozen air
fields of bitter weeds.

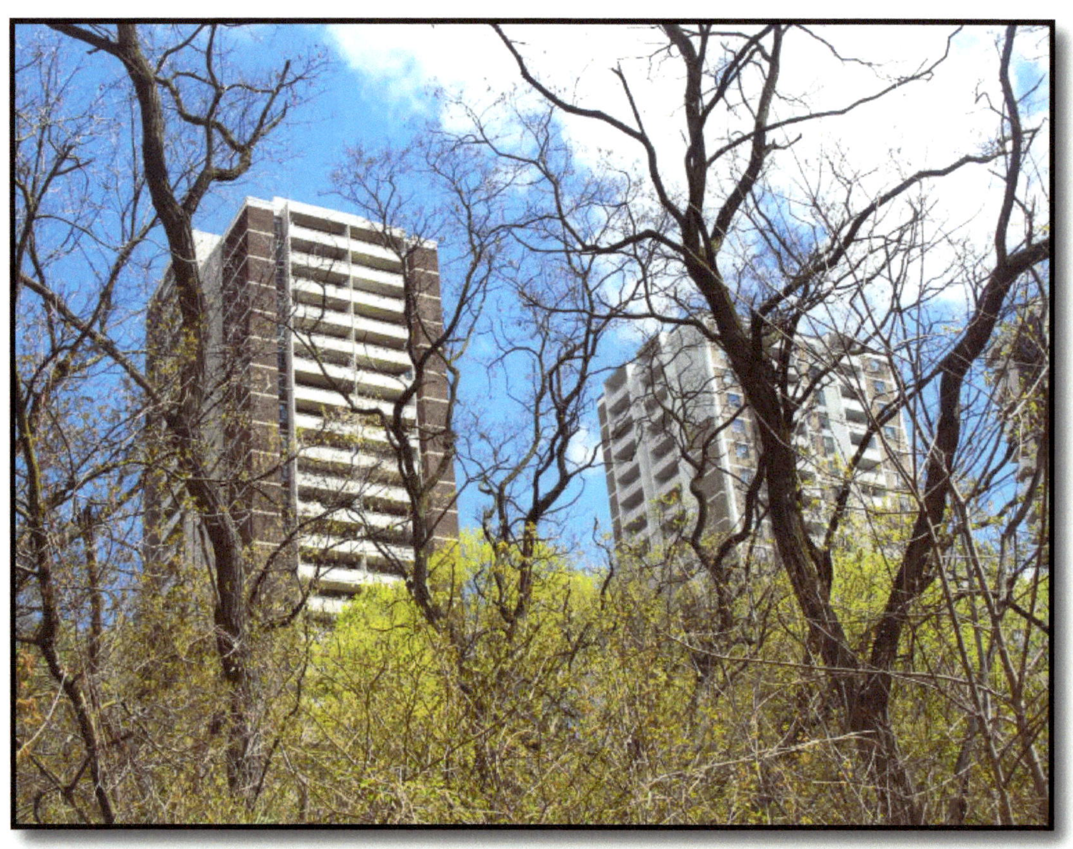

Don Valley Parkway —
thousands of cars stop and go
north in early dusk.

The first red maples
  hidden by darkness —
sharp country frost.

In utter blackness
light from a distant farm
pierces the windy night.

North of Belleville
  wild goldenrod lights up
    the harvest evening.

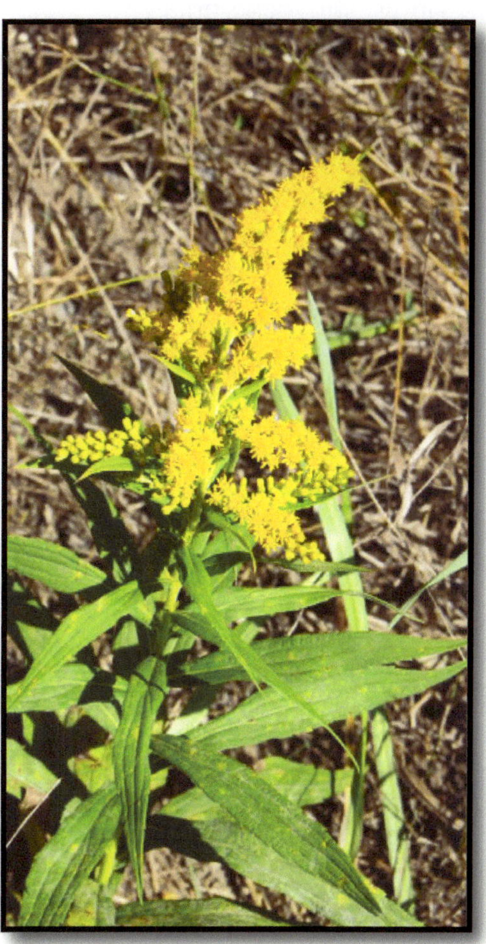

Abandoned orchard —
a single shrivelled apple
        catches the long wind.

Travelling alone
  a marsh harrier heads south
muskeg and scrub pine.

Empty school yard —
shadows gather
under autumn trees.

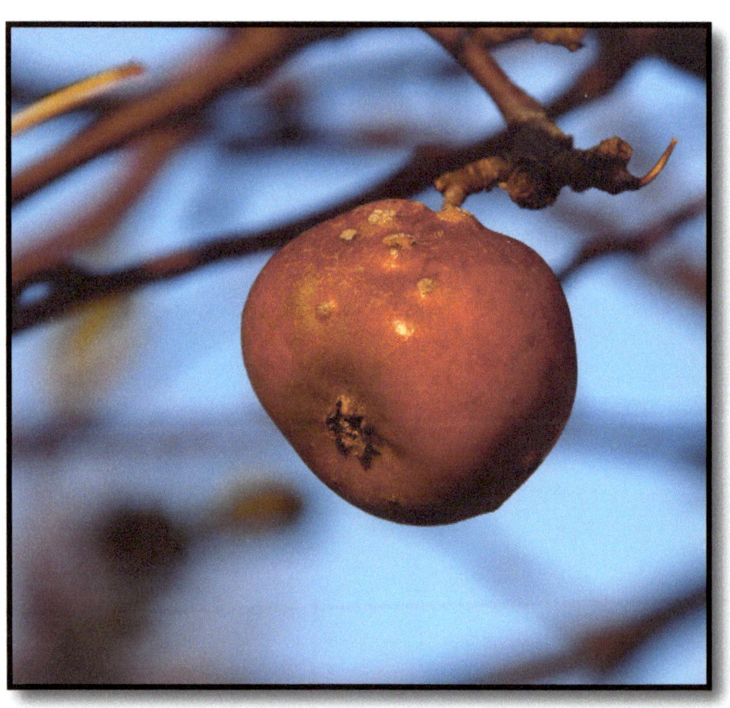

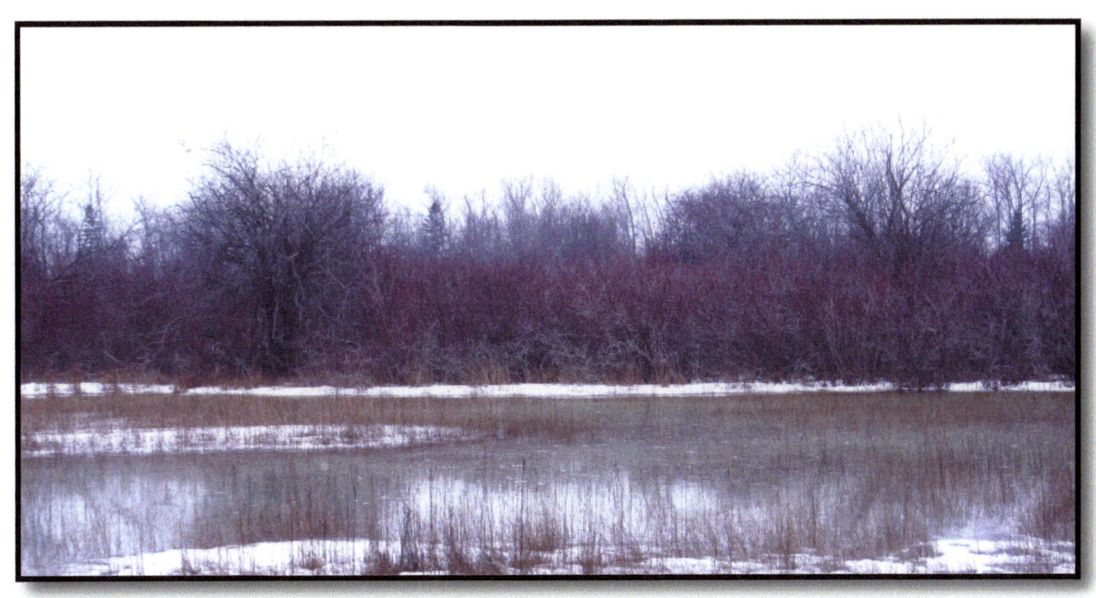

Japanese banners
    snap in November's rain —
small Ontario town.

Aftermath of storm;
the thin macadam road
    glistens into midnight.

Mississippi River
    frozen bank to bank —
        Orion strides across.

Outside the capital
white birch blown bare —
November wind.

   Arriving in Ottawa —
Osuwa festival drums
   below the Peace Tower.

   Centennial Flame —
from the shore of Lake Suwa
   sound of a *shakuhachi*.

   Crack of noon cannon
echoed by the bells of Pointe-Gatineau
    across grey water.

In the tavern
a room of middle-aged men
watch a silent TV.

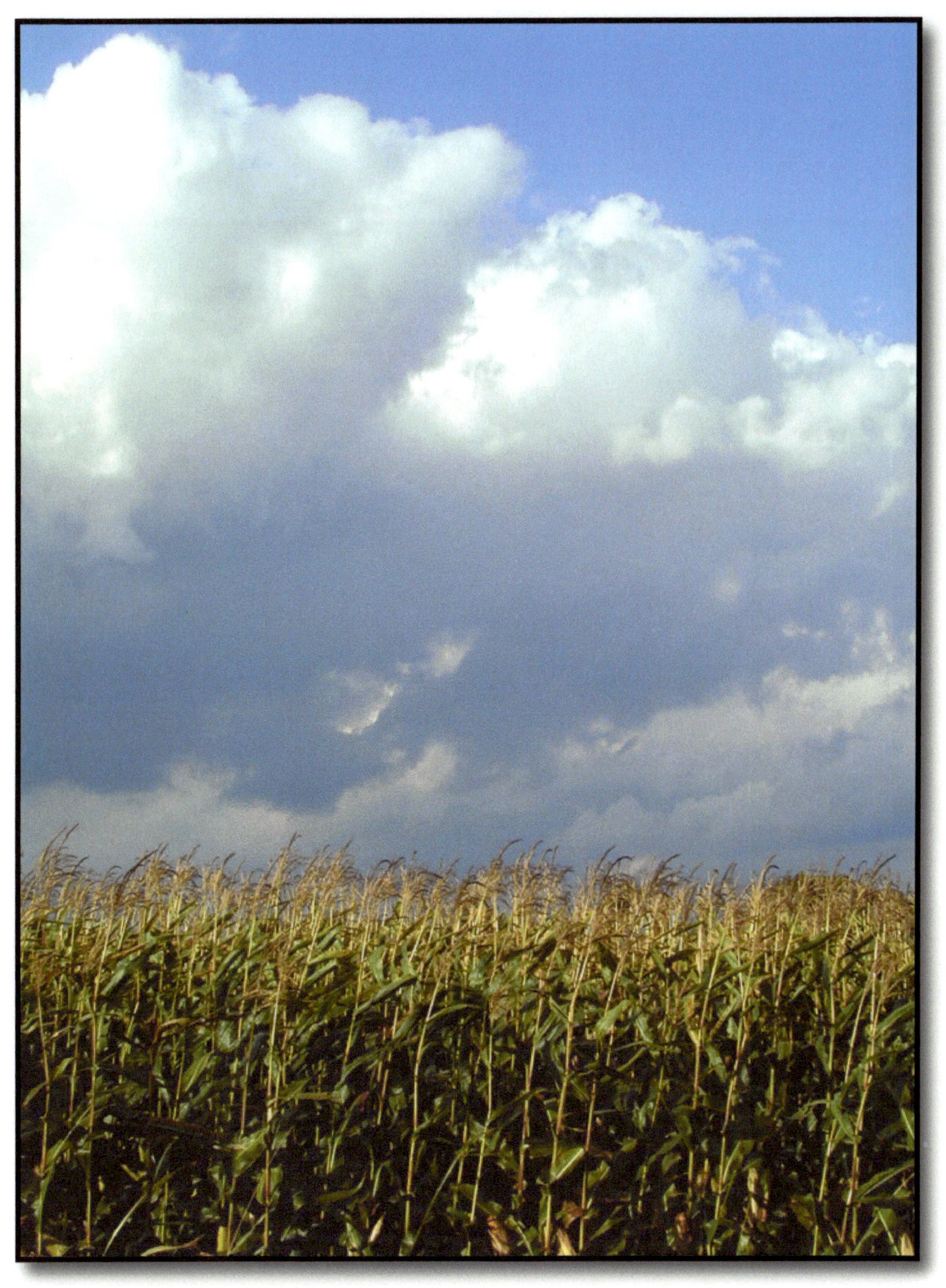

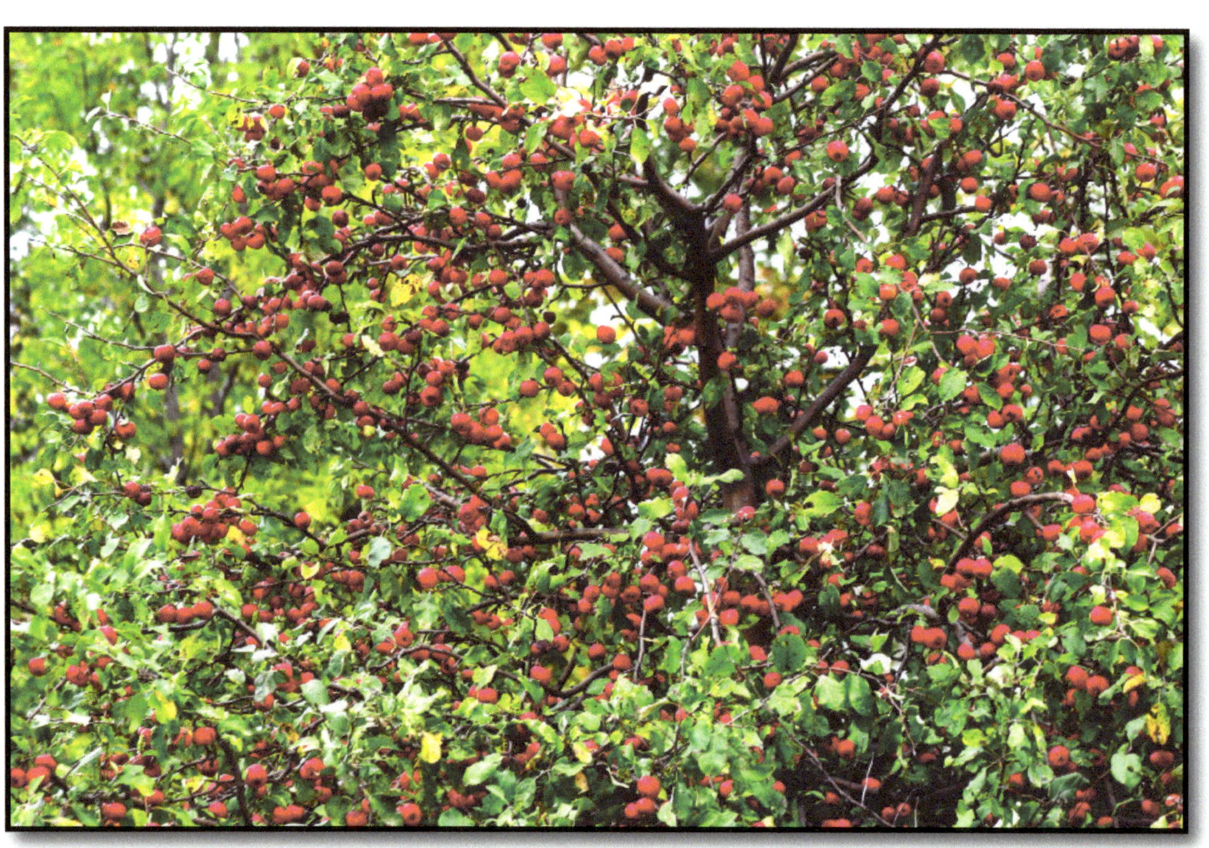

The Pinery

Close of the season —
among grass-streaked dunes
the sun low in pines.

Final westward dune,
     white pines at the fragile edge
  voice of waves below.

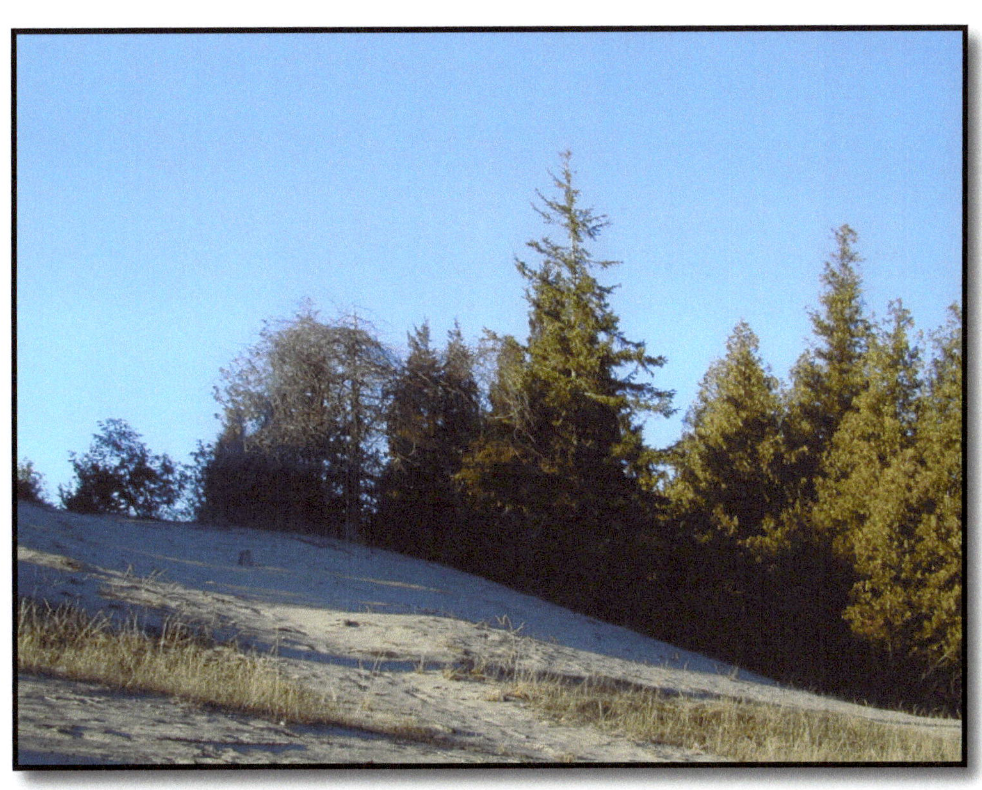

Small smoky fire;
        a beach of iron tide
steady black sound.

Mixed oak and red pine
the forest near climax —
now this evening crow.

    Fourth week of August,
a single goldenrod in tall grass —
        the whole world yellow.

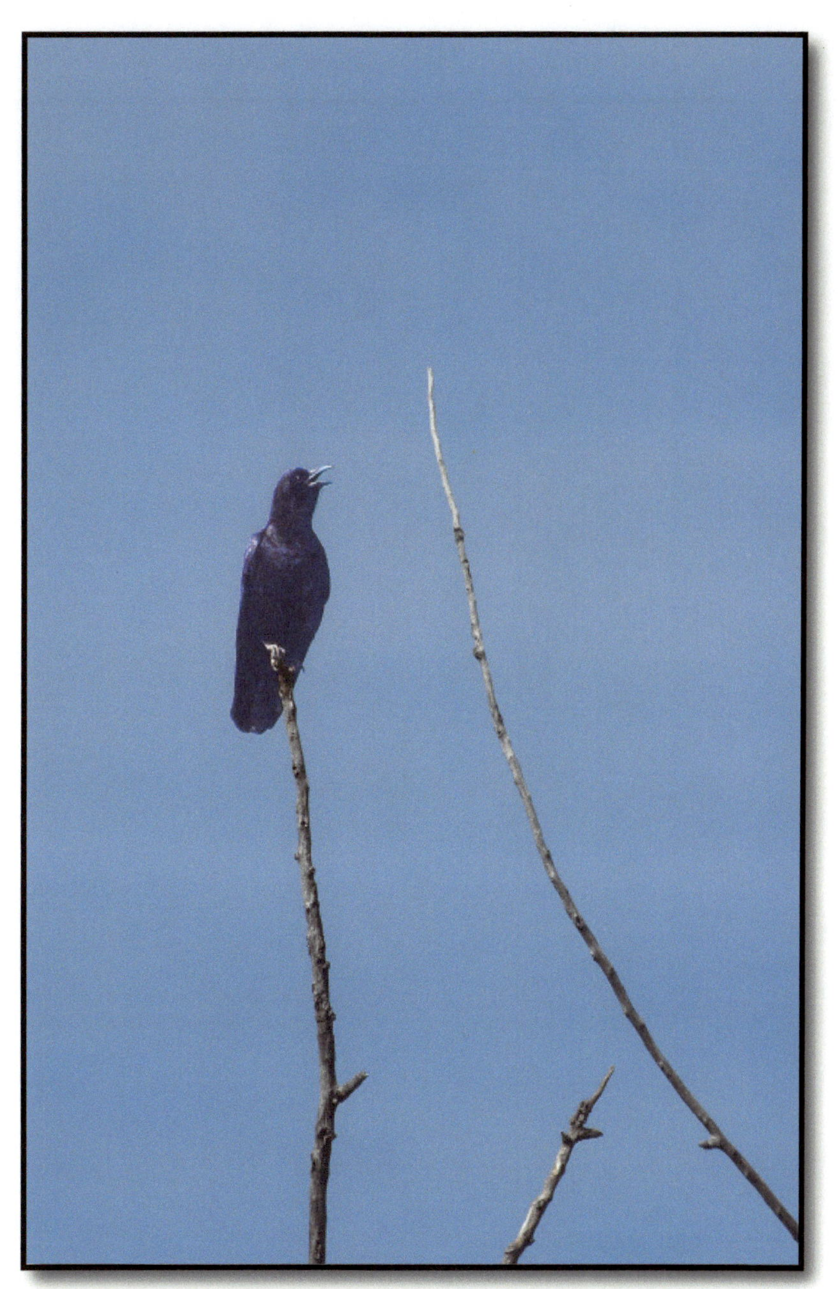

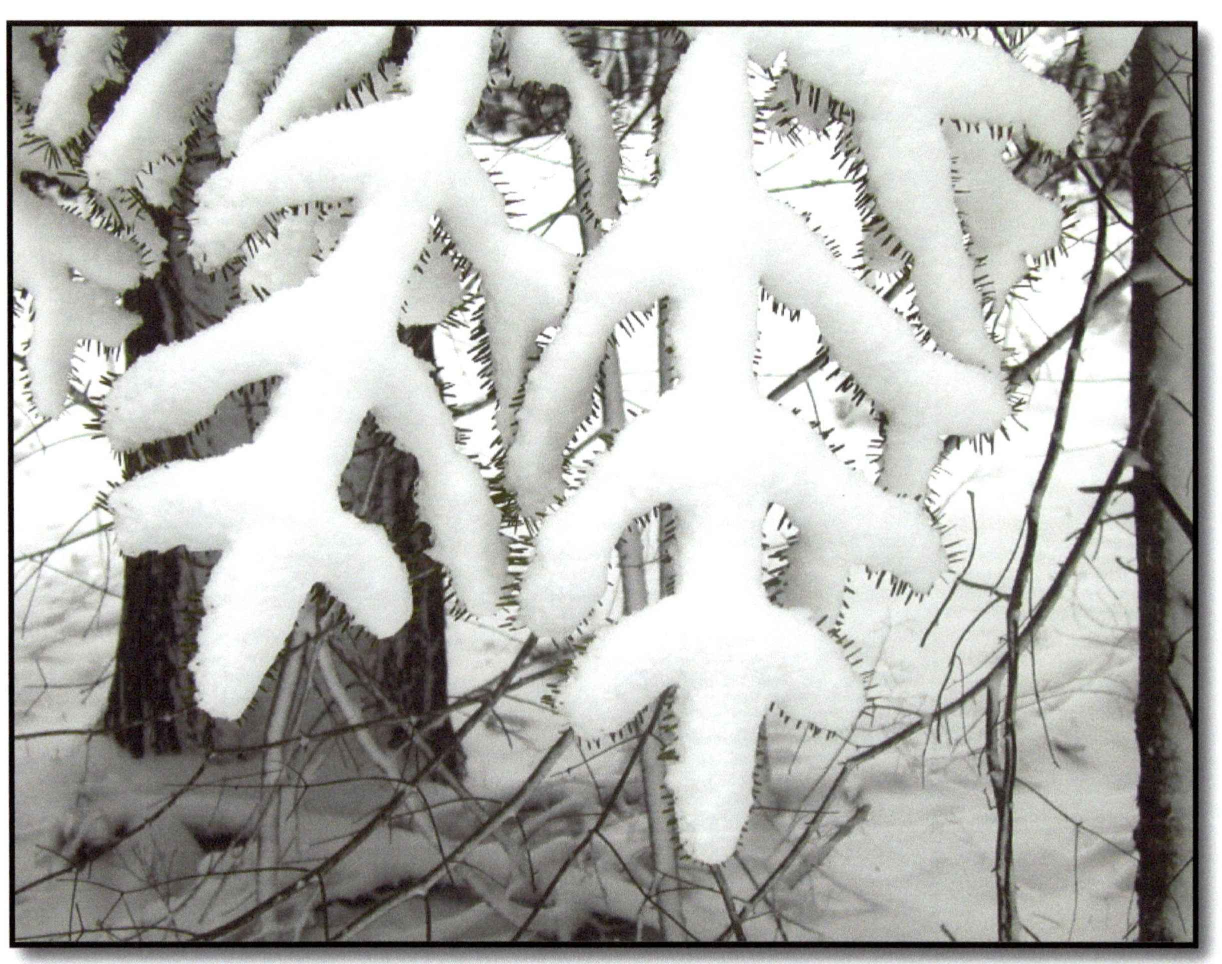

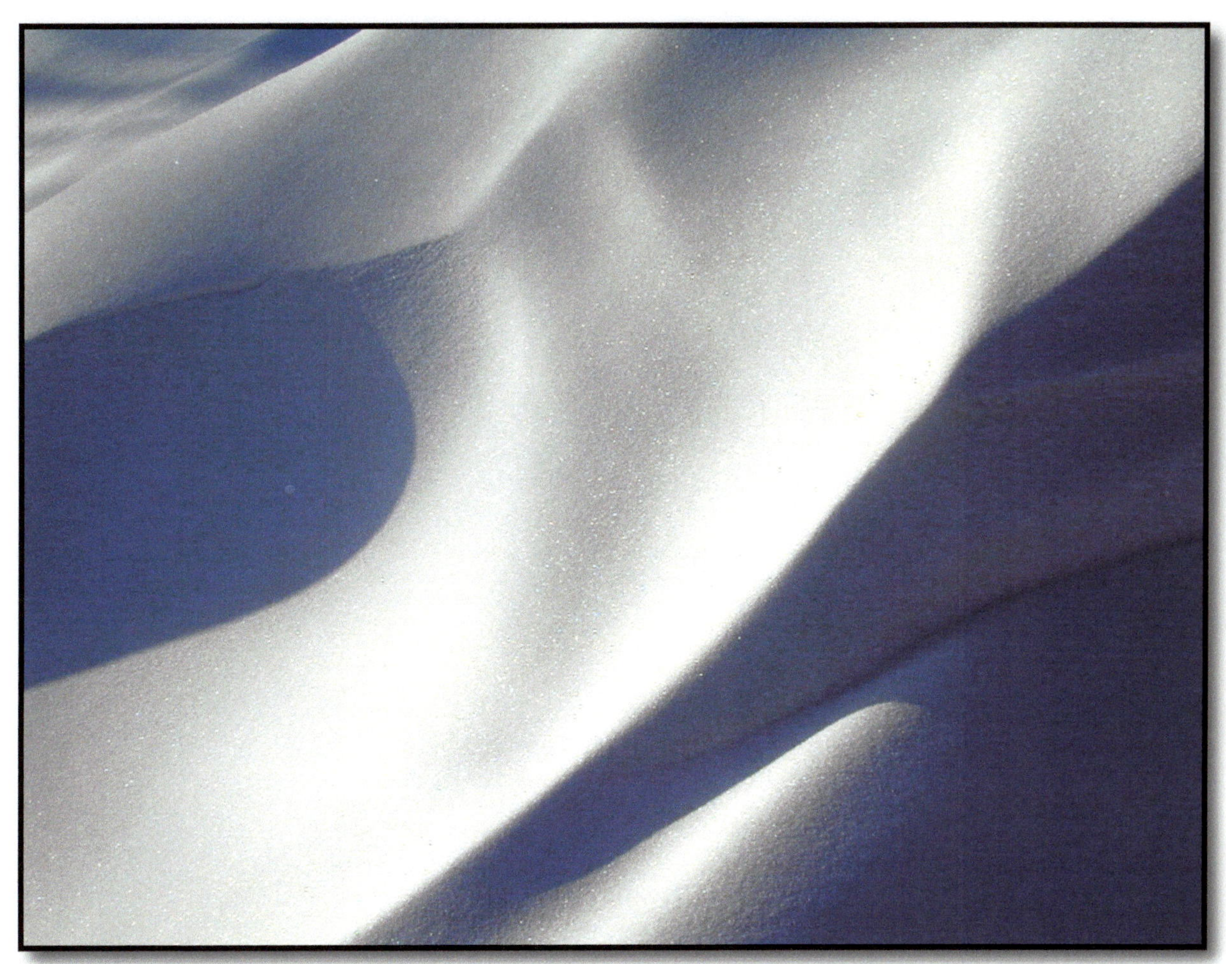

James Deahl was born in Pittsburgh (USA) in 1945, and grew up in that city as well as in and around the Laurel Highlands region of the Appalachian Mountains. He moved to Canada in 1970 and holds dual American/Canadian citizenship. He is the author (or, in the case of Tu Fu, translator) of nineteen literary titles, most recently *Opening The Stone Heart* and *No Star Is Lost*.

A poem in his first collection of haiku, *Blue Ridge*, won the Mainichi Award (Tokyo, Japan). *Tasting The Winter Grapes* won the Award of Excellence from the Hamilton & Region Arts Council. In 2001 Deahl was presented with the Charles Olson Award for Achievements in Poetry. His *When Rivers Speak* won the Ramada Plaza Hotel Award for Poetry.

For ten years, he was the managing partner of Mekler & Deahl, Publishers, Unfinished Monument Press, and hamilton haiku press. During that decade fifty books were published.

James was the international editor for *Poetry Canada Review*, the Canadian editor of the *Pittsburgh Quarterly*, and the assistant editor of *intrinsic!* magazine.

In addition to his writing, he has taught creative writing and Canadian literature at the high school (Norwell District Secondary School), college (Seneca College), and university (Ryerson University) levels. He no longer teaches, and for the past dozen years has mostly been a full-time writer/editor/translator.

James Deahl lives in Sarnia. He is the father of Sarah, Simone, and Shona.

Richard Marvin Grove was born into an artist-family in Hamilton, Ontario, on October 7, 1953. With both parents (Marvin and Ruth) being artists and art collectors he had a unique and early introduction into the world of visual art. His first experience with art was with photography when, at the age of thirteen, he purchased, with his father's enthusiasm and help, his first single lens reflex camera. Over the ensuing years, after leaving high school, he studied pottery at Mohawk College, design and pottery at Sheridan College, which led to his graduating in 1984 from the Experimental Arts Department at Ontario College of Art. In 1994 he graduated with honours from the Humber College, Arts Administration diploma course. In 2002 he returned to school to study computer courses relating to publishing.

Since graduating from Ontario College of Art, Richard has exhibited in more than twenty solo and group exhibitions in Hamilton, Toronto, Boston, Calgary and Grand Prairie. He has his art and photographs in over thirty corporate collections across Canada. The most prominent of which are Esso Resources, Continental Insurance, Alberta Energy Corporation and Calgary District Hospital Group. These four companies alone represent a collection of well over 25 pieces of his work. Among the many corporate collections are six commissions of different styles and mediums ranging from pastel on paper to acrylic on canvas.

Along with his visual art Richard has been writing poetry seriously for decades and has been published widely in periodicals and anthologies around the world. His first book of poetry titled *Beyond Fear and Anger*, was released in 1997. His second book titled *Poems For Jack*, was released in 2002 with *A View of Contrasts*, soon after that. His book of digital paintings and poetry entitled *Sky Over Presqu'ile: Fragments of Time*, was released in 2003. *Family Reunion*, a collection of short stories / novella was published in 2007. *Psycho Babble and the Consternations of Life* was released in 2008. *From Cross Hill* and *Trapped in Paradise*, both memoirs of travelling in Cuba, were published in 2009 and 2010.

He is an editor and publisher and runs Hidden Brook Press, SandCrab Books and Reflections on the Past from his home in Presqu'ile Provincial Park. He is most proud of his Canadian literary series called The North Shore Series. He is the president of the CCLA – Canada Cuba Literary Alliance - www.CanadaCubaLiteraryAlliance.org, the founding president of the Brighton Arts Council and the founding member of the Brighton and area Writers Group.

www.ingramcontent.com/pod-product-compliance
Lightning Source LLC
Chambersburg PA
CBHW042151030726
47599CB00004B/691